TIMELESS

A PARANORMAL PERSONAL HISTORY

by Bruce Olav Solheim, Ph.D.
Illustrations by Gary Dumm

2ND EDITION

Timeless: A Paranormal Personal History

By Bruce Olav Solheim, Ph.D.

Illustrations by Gary Dumm

Second Edition

ISBN: 978-0-578-64260-4

D0048206

Boots to Books
Glendora, CA 91741 USA
bootstobooks@gmail.com
www.bruceolavsolheim.com

BB
BOOTS
TO
BOOKS

DEDICATION

I dedicate this book to all my friends, relatives, and other good people who have crossed over to the other side and who have tried with great effort to make their presence known to me. For the other entities who have tried to make my acquaintance, may the forces of good in this world and beyond keep you in your place and protect us from harm.

PREFACE TO THE SECOND EDITION

Welcome back! My editor George Verongos has reformatted this book, and artists Gary and Laura Dumm have made a few changes to the front cover, spine, and back cover to give it a new look.

You might wonder why a second edition? Well, a lot has happened since the first *Timeless* book was published. For one thing, this book is now self-published, something I would recommend to any author. Why hand over your rights to someone who would take your money and then not work for you to sell your books? Second, although I'm not changing anything that I wrote in the first edition, I do want to let you know that we're all connected, including our star brothers and sisters.

Moreover, I now know that the spirit world, alien world, and the quantum world are all the same. I don't pretend to understand it all, I'm just learning like you, and would like to share. Third, I'm putting myself out there more, by not only publishing the *Timeless* trilogy, but also my comic book, *Snarc*.

My comic book was 37 years in the making and features a half-alien, half-human, all heart, anti-hero. Check it out. I'm also speaking at the Contact in the Desert conference in Indian Wells, California, the end of May 2020. I've written a research paper for MUFON (Mutual UFO Network) and conducted a survey on PTSD and alien abduction that I hope to publish. I might also be part of an alien abduction TV show coming soon. We shall see. It's important to engage on every level possible.

Fourth, my dear departed friend Gene recently told me after I seemed astonished by some recent revelations: "Is it so hard to believe one more miraculous thing when you already believe in so many extraordinary things." He always had a way of getting right to the heart of matters. We all reach boggle points, but we must break through those artificial barriers.

And fifth, I've learned a lot more from my spirit friends and have let it all hang out in the third *Timeless* book, *Timeless Trinity*. The first book was a way for me to test the waters. Now, I have dived into the deep end. I've decided that this is no time to be timid; we must be bold. I believe that good writers take risks. I take inspiration from many sources, especially fellow writers.

Mark Twain wrote: "Drop this mean and sordid and selfish devotion to the saving of your shabby little souls, and hunt up something to do that's got some dignity to it! Risk your souls! Risk them in good causes; then if you lose them, why should you care? Reform!" Twain also wrote: "Necessity is the mother of taking chances." William Faulkner provided this: "You cannot swim for new horizons until you have courage to lose sight of the shore." My favorite president, Theodore Roosevelt added: "Far better it is to dare mighty things, to win glorious triumphs, even though checkered by failure, than to take rank with those poor spirits who neither enjoy much nor suffer much, because they live in the gray twilight that knows neither victory nor defeat." I also like this from Helen Keller: "A bend in the road is not the end of the road...Unless you fail to make the turn." I admire this succinct quote from Friedrich von Schiller: "To save all we must risk all." Aristotle offered this advice: "To write well, express yourself like the common people, but think like a wise man." And finally, this comment from Arthur Miller, which seems to sum up everything: "The best work that anybody ever writes is the work that is on the verge of embarrassing him, always."

Dear reader, thank you for picking up this book, and I hope you explore the entire *Timeless* trilogy. My life story has included angels, demons, ghosts, cryptids, haunted houses, telepathy, telekinesis, mediumship, aliens, abductions, UFOs, and non-human intelligences of all kinds. I'm a very lucky human being to have had these experiences. My job now is to help shine some light on the wonder of creation and encourage your exploration. As my ancient alien spiritual advisor Anzar said recently: "Unlock your potential. Teach others to unlock their potential. Surround yourself with those who help unlock potential and who help you shine your light and not those who dim your light."

Let's get busy and remember to live forever in the light!

ACKNOWLEDGMENTS

Firstly, I want to thank my girl, Ginger. She makes everything possible. I would also like to thank Dean Radin for corresponding with me and sharing his entangled wisdom. Thank all of you for reading this book and possessing the courage to delve deeper into the realm of the paranormal. We're fellow travelers. Additionally, I would like to thank my friends Gary and Laura Dumm. Her color work and his illustrations are inspirational and their talents limitless. I must also thank my friend George Verongos for his excellent editing and production skills.

My mother helped me to accept that there are things beyond this world that can't be so easily explained. Had it not been for her, I might not have had the courage to write this book. Lastly, I would like to thank the two people who have most inspired my writing—my friend David A. Willson (author of REMF Diary and other fine books) and Norwegian playwright Henrik Ibsen. The following passage is from Ibsen's play, Ghosts, written in 1881.

"I am half inclined to think we are all ghosts. It is not only what we have inherited from our fathers and mothers that exists again in us, but all sorts of old dead ideas and all kinds of old dead beliefs and things of that kind. They are not actually alive in us; but there they are dormant, all the same, and we can never be rid of them. Whenever I take up a newspaper and read it, I fancy I see ghosts creeping between the lines. There must be ghosts all over the world. They must be as countless as the grains of the sands, it seems to me. And we are so miserably afraid of the light, all of us."

Just as a reminder to my readers, the stories in this book reflect my recollection of events. Some names, locations, and identifying characteristics have been changed to protect the privacy of those depicted. Dialogue has been re-created from memory.

TABLE OF CONTENTS

PROLOGUE 1

POLIOMYELITIS AND THE ANGEL 7

THE BLUE BOY 13

DECEPTION PASS...19

LET'S DO LUNCH 23

UNCOMFORTABLY NUMB 29

PLEIKU ON THE LINE...31

THE TOUCH 33

MEDIC! 37

OPEN CASKET 43

HELL IS EMPTY 45

THE MOUNTAIN NYMPH...49

THAT OLD BLACK MAGIC...55

THE HILLS ARE ALIVE 65

THOUGHT LOG 75

THE TWIN ANGELS...87

GOLDEN MOM 93

NAMELESS 97

COFFEE CUPS AND VIKINGS 101

WILLY..113

METEORITE...143

ME AND MRS. COLBY 147

A HERO'S JOURNEY HOME 157

FLIGHT 77 167

SASQUATCH 171

BREATHE EASY 175

IT'S ALL TRUE 179

THE EPIPHANY 185

EPILOGUE 189

ABOUT THE ARTIST 199

BLURBS 201

PROLOGUE

It's not that I believe in ghosts, it's that they believe in me, so I've no choice. Having experienced ghosts, I've come to understand that death isn't an end, it's a doorway. So, what proof do I have? I don't have proof, I have my personal experiences, not only with life beyond death but also with many other seemingly unexplainable, paranormal phenomena that have occurred over the years. Paranormal is usually defined as something beyond the range of normal experience or scientific explanation. Parapsychologists, who aren't deterred by skeptics calling their discipline of parapsychology a pseudoscience, have successfully studied many paranormal phenomena, including:

1. Telepathy: communicating thoughts or feelings between two people not using the five traditional senses.
2. Precognition: Perceiving information about future events before they happen.
3. Clairvoyance: Gaining information about places or events at remote locations.
4. Psychokinesis: The ability of the mind to manipulate matter, time, space, or energy.
5. Near-death experiences: An experience reported by a person who came close to death, or who experienced clinical death and then was brought back to life.
6. Reincarnation: The rebirth of a soul or human consciousness in a new physical body after death.
7. Apparitional experiences: Phenomena relating to ghosts of deceased persons in places they frequented or with their belongings.

According to parapsychologist Dr. Dean Radin in his book *The Conscious Universe*, "...those compelling, perplexing, and sometimes profound human experiences known as 'psychic phenomena' are real...it has taken more than a century to demonstrate it conclusively in accordance with rigorous, scientific standards." Although my purpose in this book isn't to prove or disprove scientific theories of what Dr. Radin prefers to call psi phenomena, my personal stories will touch on many of the paranormal or psi phenomena listed above.

The experiences in this book are my own, they did happen, and I make no other claims. So, the story begins, with me, as it does with anyone. This book is a memoir, but it's a memoir of the paranormal experiences I've had. We've all thought about what happens when a person dies since our ancestors lived in caves. Although we're all unique in our own ways, birth and death are what unite all of us. Most people have a fear of death, in fact, it's the number two fear in most surveys, with public speaking being number one. So, it stands to reason that speaking in public about death would not be easy. People have been reporting paranormal events since the beginning of recorded time, but scientists have disagreed about the existence of these phenomena and many skeptics mock those people who see ghosts or have paranormal experiences. Yet, paranormal stories hold considerable interest worldwide. It's one of those things that ties all of us together, all cultures, everywhere in the world.

This book does not claim to have all the answers as to why paranormal phenomena occur nor can I help people get in contact with their dead relatives or friends, I wish I could. I experience paranormal events frequently, but randomly. I'm just relating my experiences that I believe are shared by many people around the world. I'm not out to take people's hard-earned money by playing on their emotions or manipulating those who are grief-stricken. I hope this book will, however, inspire people not to be afraid of the unknown and help them connect to a part of themselves that is unexplored and share those experiences with others and to encourage scientists to continue their research. I do offer some possible explanations and theories, but they are only meant to further discussion not prove or disprove anything. I'm not a professional paranormal researcher, a scientist, or a psychologist. Although I do hold a Ph.D. in history and have published several books, I'm simply a person who has experienced many unusual paranormal events and have always been fascinated by those experiences and would like to share them with others.

Consider this: Ancient people lived in a world populated with both real and ethereal beings. Now we could dismiss this by saying that ancient people were superstitious, uneducated simpletons, or we could honor and learn from our ancestors by trying to understand their world. It's my view that there are ethereal beings among us, but, for most people, their modern senses don't recognize them, and skeptics take comfort when scientists continue to disagree about the existence of paranormal or psi phenomena. For those people who have had significant paranormal events in their lives, it's not a matter of belief, as in religion, it's a matter of actual experience. Some embrace this gift, others shun it as a curse, and perhaps even some are driven mad. Joseph Campbell, in his Power of Myth video series, shared a story about a discussion he had with a Catholic priest. After Joseph told the priest of his life's work studying world religions and mythology, the priest said:

"It sounds like you are a man of faith Joseph." Joseph Campbell looked at him and said:

"I don't need faith; I have experience."

This book was 58 years in the making, being that it's my life story. I've had many unusual events and experiences in my life, some good, some not, but all of them seem to point to something that isn't easy to explain and opens new ways of looking at the world. Having been raised as a Norwegian Lutheran, I assumed that all my questions about these paranormal events and experiences could be answered through religion. At age 9, I remember fervently praying one Sunday at Northlake Lutheran Church in Kenmore, Washington. I was praying to ask God to help my Pee Wee football team win our championship game. I was hoping and praying that if God could somehow see his way clear to ensure our victory then I would be happy, and all would be right with the universe. We won our championship, but later I was not sure if it was God's intervention or our strong offensive line and running game that led to our victory that day. I began to have doubts. When my parents left the church a year later because dad did not want to pay what the church committee asked him to pay and because the same committee fired our beloved pastor, my doubts grew stronger. Did God have a hand in this or was he unable to help? The questions only got bigger and more in number as I grew older, and the unusual events continued.

As a kid, I remember lying on my back in the yard and looking up at the sky thinking that we must live in the belly of a giant. When he drank, it rained. Maybe, I thought, I'm also a giant, and there was a world inside my stomach too. I think it was those thoughts that led me to believe that we were not alone in the universe and opened me up to considering many imaginative possibilities. Chronologically, the following stories document actual paranormal experiences that I've had throughout my life. It's time to put aside our fears and share our stories with each other. I'm reminded of a line in Shakespeare's *Hamlet*.

"There are more things in heaven and earth, Horatio, than are dreamt of in your philosophy," said Hamlet in *Hamlet*, Act 1, Scene 5. I hope you enjoy my stories and open yourself to the

4

experience of seeing, hearing, feeling, and sensing in every possible way the unknown.

POLIOMYELITIS AND THE ANGEL

My first big adventure was in 1962 when we drove across the United States and then took an ocean liner from New York to Oslo, Norway. There was a World's Fair in Seattle when we left in 1962. It was a big deal; even Elvis was there. We (myself, my brother, my mom, and my dad) traveled across the United States in a two-tone blue 1959 Ford station wagon. I was not yet four years old during our trip across America, but I do remember the scary thunderstorms and hail in Montana and getting on the ship in New York. We had loaded our car and our belongings on board the ship and stood on the deck by the railing waving to the crowd as the ship shoved off. Mom was so excited about returning to Norway that she dropped her sunglasses into the harbor. Dad made me laugh when he said that there would now be some fish swimming around wearing mom's sunglasses. We traveled on the Stavangerfjord, part of the Norwegian American Line. It was the same ship that my parents and my sister were on when they immigrated in 1948. Our return voyage would be the last one for Stavangerfjord (built in 1917) because it was sold for scrap a year later.

I had free run of the ship. And, in those days parents did not hover over their children like they do today. I remember running through the engine room and being chased by crew members. I would dangle from the back railing of the ship (like in the *Titanic* movie). It was a miracle that I lived through the voyage there and back. When I was hungry, I would help myself to food from the galley. I remember that one of the stewards showed me the mechanical cow that made our milk on board the ship. I was very impressed. Most of the time I was always one step ahead of the crew as they searched for the kid who had run amok. Despite that, the crew treated kids very well. They called me Master Bruce. Oh, by the way, my mom wanted to name me after Roy Rogers, her favorite singing cowboy, but my dad insisted on Bruce. The eleven-day trip across the Atlantic was great except for two stormy days. For two days, we were not allowed to go on deck because of the weather. Everyone seemed worried, but I used the time to explore beneath the decks.

When we got to Norway, we drove our Ford station wagon all the way up North having to take many ferries to get to the island of Andøya, two hundred miles above the Arctic Circle. We lived with my grandmother (my father's mother). My grandfather had already passed away. In fact, she was the only grandparent that I ever met. I loved living in the little village of Åse, and my grandmother (named Mimmi) spoiled me rotten. We lived with her for nine months, and I still remember Christmas in her house with a real tree with real candles. I also remember that the snow was very deep. When we got to Norway, we got to see the house where my mom was born just before it was bulldozed to the ground. Grandmother had died just before we arrived. I remember my mom crying and holding some of the possessions that she had salvaged from the house. Soon it was fall, and in October 1962 during the Cuban Missile Crisis, my parents were extremely worried. Mom called the US Embassy in Oslo, and they told her to listen to the radio and stay in touch in case something happened. Mom and dad had had enough of war, but then it always seemed to come back around.

As much as I enjoyed living with my grandmother, it was hard on my parents. My grandma was one to spoil children, and especially me. One time I had done something bad and dad wanted to spank me. My grandma grabbed me from my father.

"If you spank this child, then you will be the next one to get spanked," she said. She was a perfect grandma. She even liked to look at *MAD* magazine, although sometimes she had the annoying habit of tearing the pages out to use as toilet paper in the outhouse. The island in northern Norway was a winter paradise. I often rode on my grandma's sled. This sled was called a *spark* in Norwegian. It looked like a chair with long runners. My grandma would put me in the spark and slide us down to the village market for food. It was an idyllic life for a kid.

The Northern Norwegians live in darkness for three months in the winter. They call it, *The Dark Time.* One day I came home and had a terrible headache, muscle aches, extreme fatigue, and my neck was feeling stiff. I laid down in a little bed in the kitchen. I fell asleep and when I woke up it was difficult to move my arms and legs and my neck was completely stiff. I was very sick and had a high fever. There was no hospital on the island, and my parents were worried out of their minds.

One of our cousins from next door came over and told my grandmother that the same thing happened to her son in the late 1940s and he was paralyzed for life by polio. Then someone said that my older brother, named Bjørn, got sick very quickly during the war and died in just one day. He was only two years old. This story frightened everyone especially me. I remember staring up at the beams in the ceiling in the kitchen crying and not being able to move while everyone tried not to seem too panicky around me. I prayed that I would not die that night or be paralyzed.

I somehow was able to get to sleep despite my fear and pain. I woke up in that little bed in the kitchen and saw an angel up in the ceiling beams above me. The angel was in a glowing human form like she was made of light. I felt warm, calm, peaceful, and wasn't afraid. I knew the angel was real and I wasn't dreaming. The next day when I woke up, I was fine. My arms and legs moved, my headache was gone, and my neck was no longer stiff. Was it the prayer? Was it the angel? Was it just a temporary condition caused by the extreme cold? My mom and my grandmother said it was a miracle and that I had a guardian angel watching over me. I believe it was a miracle and it would not be the first time that there was a miraculous intervention in my life.

THE BLUE BOY

I saw death for the first time in 1964. I had seen someone who was near death when my parents, in their infinite wisdom, took me to see a relative who was dying of lung cancer. The pain and suffering I saw frightened me away from smoking cigarettes or anything else. Mom always reminded me of the harm done by smoking and alcohol.

"Don't smoke and don't drink," she said. She had lost her father to alcoholism when he committed suicide by hanging himself in the attic of her childhood home in Northern Norway. My mom was just a young girl when my grandfather took his own life. The experience I had in 1964, however, still haunts me today and taught me a valuable lesson.

The Sons of Norway Leif Erikson Lodge, in Seattle, was a big part of my life growing up. I remember going to Christmas parties and other events as a very young boy. Then, in 1963, the Sons of Norway purchased an old farm property in Lake McMurray, Washington. They called the place *Norway Park,* and the *Sons of Norway* sold cabin lots. The property was divided by old State Route 9. The lower half of the abandoned farm was beachfront, and the upper half was for cabin lots. My parents were one of the first families to buy into the park. We had Lot 209 on Drammens Alle. Our lot had a large tree stump from an old growth tree. The stump was probably 13 feet in diameter. We built a ladder to get up to the top of the stump which was about 12 feet high. The stump was hollow, so we could also climb down into it and play inside. My dad hooked up a rope swing in the steep entryway to our lot. It was a kid's paradise. We started camping at our lot on a regular basis. Other lot owners began to build cabins, but my parents just wanted to camp in a canvas tent that connected to our station wagon and later with their camper. To get down to the lake, we had to cross State Route 9 and an old railroad track that was rarely used. During the heyday of logging in the area, that railway ran day and night. We used to walk a mile or so down the tracks toward the McMurray store. Along the way, we passed by the abandoned saw mill. The mill still had a big saw blade, rusted out, under a building that was partially collapsed and sitting on rotted pilings. At the lake, my dad and the other men built a dock and a diving board. On the Fourth of July 1964, there was a big party down by the lake and a salmon barbecue put on by the *McMurray Volunteer Fire Department*. A lot of the adults were drinking heavily. I've never liked being around people who are drunk, nothing good ever seems to happen when people are inebriated. I remember having an eerie feeling that day. While the adults were partying, a young boy, maybe five years old, went missing. His older brother was supposed to watch him, but he decided to go down to the lake and left his little brother at the cabin. I remember that everyone was in a panic looking for the boy. The search parties were calling the little boy's name as they combed the woods by the cabin lots, crisscrossed the lake in row boats, and even drove down to the Lake McMurray Store. My mom and dad and I were helping with the search.

"I think I see him in water," I told my dad.

"What do you mean? Did you see him go into the water?" asked my father.

"No, I just think he's in the water, shallow water," I said. My dad told the other people, and we focused on the swimming area around the dock because that was where all the kids would swim. No one had thought to look there because there were always so many people swimming by the dock. An older Norwegian-American man, who was known as a drunk, was walking on the dock when he spotted something. He dove in with all his clothes on and came out with the little boy in his arms.

"Oh, my God," said my mom. The crowd gasped, the mother and father of the boy were crying, and calls were made for an ambulance. The man who found the boy laid him down on the grass and they started doing mouth to mouth resuscitation and chest compressions. One of the volunteer firefighters took over, but it was too late. The boy had been missing for 30 minutes at least. I joined the circle around the little boy, who was the same age as me. I noticed that the little boy was blue.

"Is he dead?" I asked. Several people told me to be quiet.

"I think so," dad said.

"Let's go, let them try to help him," my mom said as she dragged me away. I watched the man who found the little boy continue to try to resuscitate him. He was crying in anguish. I remember dad telling me that the drunk man who found the boy had fought against the Nazis in World War II as a member of the Resistance in Norway. He was a war hero. The little boy's parents knelt beside the boy in shock. The look on the little boy's face bothered me even more than the blue color of his skin. His face was tranquil, like a newborn baby. There was no sign of horror, of pain, of struggle, nothing. The boy was already gone, and the people around him continued to live. His life was over. As my mom continued to drag me away, I could not help watching the scene and hoping the little boy would rise, cough, and be okay. That did not happen.

"What happens when you die?" I asked my mom.

"You go to heaven if you are a good person and believe in God," she said.

"Did that little boy believe in God?" I asked.

"I'm sure he did," answered mom.

My mom stopped to talk to another lady, and I looked back once more at the scene of death. I did not hear any voices, only silence; time seemed to stand still. It appeared to me that death does not wait for understanding. Death could come slow or swift in equal measure. Would the little blue boy still look the same and stay the same age in heaven? Do we remember who we are when we go to heaven? What happens to our consciousness and our memories? Are they like windless kites that fall to the ground? I had so many questions, but few answers. We all march forward in uncertainty, yet we all know that the march forward will end at some point. When will it end? Nobody knows. My friend James Wire, who was a Pearl Harbor survivor, told me that he joined the Navy in World War II because he thought that dying at sea would be a clean death as opposed to dying in some muddy trench. I respect the ocean, lakes, rivers, and any body of water. I never enter the water without thinking about the little blue boy and life and death and the narrow separation between them.

DECEPTION PASS

Another one of my earliest memories was of an incident that happened in 1965 on a family camping trip to a place called *Deception Pass State Park* (in Washington State) when I was nearly seven years old. There are two ways to get to Deception Pass. One way was to take a ferry to the south end of Whidbey Island and then drive to the north end to arrive at Deception Pass. The other way was to drive up Interstate 5 to Burlington and then go West toward Anacortes and drive on to Whidbey Island via two bridges from Fidalgo Island to Pass Island (in the middle) and then finally to Whidbey Island. The two bridge spans aren't very long—one is only 500 feet, and the other is 1000 feet. The drop to the dangerous waters below is nearly 200 feet. The waters at Deception Pass at tide change are so turbulent because it's a narrow, deep channel that connects the Strait of Juan de Fuca with the Saratoga Passage. More than 500 people have committed suicide at Deception Pass since the 1930s by jumping off the bridge spans. Maybe that's why the bridge always gave me a rather eerie feeling. We would stop at Pass Island, where there was a small parking lot, and would get out to look around and marvel at the great height and rugged beauty of this unique Pacific Northwest location. There were plenty of trails on Pass Island, and none of them were supervised or had any protective safety fences or guard rails in 1965. It was very treacherous with a lot of sharp rocks below the steep high cliffs on the north side of Pass Island, (called Canoe Pass).

One summer day I remember running around like crazy, like I usually did when I was a kid, with my parents not knowing where I was half the time. As I was running with careless abandon down a trail on the north side of *Pass Island*, I didn't notice that the path ended abruptly at the edge of the cliff. The cliff plunged down nearly vertical with sharp rocks at the bottom 200 feet below in the raging, turbulent seawater running through the narrow channel. I've two memories of what happened next. In one memory, I plunged to my certain death alone and immediately knew what a terrible mistake I had made. Oddly, I don't remember hitting the rocks below, just blackness. In another memory, I ran off the cliff and again knew I was doomed, but then time stood still as I floated in the air momentarily. I felt an intense warmth and bright light hovering near me and holding me. The next thing I knew, I was back on the trail as if nothing had happened. My dad had me by the shoulders. He was furious and yelled at me. My mom came after and was crying. Had I fallen from the cliff and died or had some mysterious force or entity stopped the tragedy and safely lifted me back on to the trail? Obviously, I'm writing these words, so I must have lived, yet, I have this haunting feeling that something else happened as well. My parents were very angry and never spoke about this incident. I was convinced that this was the work of my guardian angel once again.

I've thought about this near-death experience over the years and wonder if sometimes different paths in our lives run simultaneously. In other words, maybe there is one version where I died and another version where I lived. Maybe these forks in the road of time happen every once in a while, and therefore we never really die we just continue living on another path ad infinitum. Eventually, after we experience many such forks, we finally reach old age and die, but only temporarily. Maybe we then return anew to start another life—reincarnated. It's just a theory; I've no proof, just a hunch. Perhaps there is no death, and perhaps death is the greatest deception of all.

LET'S DO LUNCH

I know it seems strange and maybe even a little creepy that an 8-year-old boy would like to hang around graveyards, but I loved visiting *Abbey View Cemetery* near my home in Kenmore, Washington. The cemetery was a little more than a mile from my house. I even got my friend Tommy interested, and we would go together. His brother Johnny refused. We would pack our lunches and ride our bikes up to the cemetery. There was a tall statue of Jesus that would greet us as we rode up the driveway to the headstones. Sometimes, Tommy would feel uncomfortable about being in the graveyard.

"Are you sure we should be here?" he asked.

"Yeah, why not," I said.

"I don't know, seems weird," he said.

"They have these graveyards, so folks will visit," I explained.

"Yeah, but would Jesus like it, that we're here I mean?" he asked with some apprehension as he looked at the giant sad-faced statue of Jesus.

"Oh sure, he loves it. He'll protect us. Especially since we're usually the only ones here," I answered assuredly.

"Nobody else is here because they're smart," said Tommy, who was Catholic and crossed himself just for good measure.

"Hey, do you remember the song?" I asked.

"What song?" asked Tommy.

"You know, the one we always sing when we see a funeral go by when we're outside playing in your yard," I said.

"Never laugh when a hearse goes by," I sang.

"Stop it, that's bad luck," said Tommy.

"Or you will be the next to die," I continued, then laughed.

"You're just mean," said Tommy.

In the summer, we would ride up to *Abbey View Cemetery* for lunch at least once a week. We found soldier graves and old headstones too. We liked hanging out in the oldest, scariest part of the graveyard.

"Aren't you afraid?" asked Tommy as he adjusted his taped, black, horn-rimmed glasses.

"Nah, I like it here. It's peaceful," I said.

"What about ghosts?" asked Tommy nervously.

"Only at night, I think," I said. I enjoyed eating lunch at *Abbey View*. I loved the peace and quiet as we sat underneath the trees by the headstones. I felt very comfortable, and I thought it was a good place to think.

One Summer day, after riding our bikes throughout the late afternoon and early evening, we decided to explore the area around the mortuary office building on the other side of the street. My brother Alf said that there was a lake below the mortuary that he and his friends had explored. The mortuary building was where they did the cremations, and the morticians and grave-diggers had their main office. We rode our bikes down the dirt road around the back of the building, through the forest, and headed toward the lake. As it turned out, it was more of a pond than a lake, but it was a big pond. There were tall trees with creeping ivy around the perimeter of the pond standing like silent, spooky sentinels. We also saw thousands of lily pads and other green stuff floating on the water. We decided to call it a swamp pond. There was a mist starting to rise from the swamp pond, as the sun was starting to go down and the tall trees already block the light. By the near shore, there were large cement crypts stacked here and there. Some of the crypts were overgrown with blackberry bushes. We could hear the sounds of crickets and an occasional bull frog.

"Looks like this is where the creature from the Black Lagoon would live," I said. Tommy was already scared and didn't appreciate my humor.

"Stop it! We gotta get outta here!" he yelled.

"Let's look around some more," I said. Tommy stayed with me, probably because he didn't want to ride back up the dirt road through the darkening forest by himself.

We looked at the crypts more closely and found some old beer bottles broken inside of them.

"Probably the bad boys and girls were here," I said.

"Yeah, maybe," said Tommy nervously, looking all around.

"That looks like a bloody handprint on this one," I said.

"No, it's not," said Tommy as I laughed. Then, the crickets stopped chirping, and the bull frogs stopped croaking as there was an odd noise from the other side of the swamp pond.

"What's that?!" asked Tommy.

"I don't know," I answered. Whatever it was, it was pretty big.

"Okay, we looked around enough, let's go, it's gettin' dark," said Tommy. The mist was getting denser and rising up from the surface of the swamp pond giving off a very spooky aura. Then, the sound of something crashing through the bushes on the other side of the swamp pond echoed across the murky water. Tommy hopped on his bike and took off like a shot.

"Let's get the hell outta here!" he yelled over his shoulder.

"Wait," I said. My chain had come off when I started to peddle my bike. The crashing noise was getting closer, like the sound of snapping branches and twigs and heavy footsteps. We could see the bushes moving violently as the sound came even closer to us. Tommy had stopped to look back.

"It's some kinda creature! Come on! Are you crazy?!" he asked.

"My chain fell off!" I yelled. I was panicking, but finally, I got the chain back on the main gear. The creature was now on our side of the lake and closing in on us. We could hear grunting and snarling noises along with the heavy footsteps and sounds of branches snapping under its weight.

"Oh my God!" screamed Tommy, as he peddled as fast as he could to get away. I peddled as if my life depended on it because it probably did. I looked back over my shoulder to see if the creature was coming for us. The mist had taken over the shore of the swamp pond and was moving up over the crypts. The sounds had stopped, and I could see a shadowy figure standing near the crypts in the mist but couldn't make out any features. Whatever it was, it stood on two legs. We peddled up to the main road and didn't stop or look back until we were home. Tommy was out of breath, and so was I when we got to his house.

"What was that thing?" he asked.

"I don't know, but I'm never going down to that swamp pond any more," I answered.

"Or the graveyard," Tommy added. I never got Tommy to go back with me to the cemetery, but I did go there a few more times, by myself. After the incident with the swamp pond creature, I didn't feel as comfortable and peaceful when I sat by myself eating lunch at *Abbey View*.

One day, as I sat there by myself, I looked over to the giant statue of Jesus. Maybe he had some answers I thought. He just stood there in sad-faced silence, his right arm by his side, and the left arm raised with his hand and index finger pointing toward the swamp pond. I hadn't noticed that before, and it gave me a jolt. Was he acknowledging the creature and warning me? I never returned to the swamp pond.

UNCOMFORTABLY NUMB

I've always been afraid of going to the doctor or dentist, and I'm naturally terrified of hospitals. When I was younger, we had a family doctor who made house calls. His name was Dr. Phil Gardner. He was the doctor who delivered my brother and me. A few times a year, when I was a young boy, I would get sick and then go to sleep and wake up struggling to breathe. My air passages would tighten, and I would cough. I sounded like a baby seal, but I eventually grew out of it. Dr. Gardner called it croup, and it terrified me every time it happened.

When I was 11 years old, I became very sick and thought for sure that I was going to get croup again. It didn't happen, but I did get a very high fever, maybe 105 degrees Fahrenheit. It might have been the 1968 Hong Kong Flu pandemic that killed millions around the world, but at that time, my concern was not a pandemic, but my growing delirium. I can remember becoming disassociated, and as I watched a show on our old black and white television, it seemed as though the heads on the screen were growing larger. I was frightened, but then, if that wasn't bad enough, I started to feel like my hands were growing larger. It was freaking me out. I looked at them, and they appeared normal, but I had the sensation that they were growing larger and larger and floating up into the air like balloons. I had to tuck my hands under my butt so that I could stop the feeling. I still remember it vividly. This incident was another time when I felt like maybe I had died because it was so surreal.

Some 30 years later I was listening to Pink Floyd, and I finally paid careful attention to the lyrics from the song, *Comfortably Numb*. Roger Waters sang about what I had gone through.

When I was a child I had a fever.

My hands felt just like two balloons.

I know exactly what he meant, and I know exactly how he felt. I've read that when people are dying, they hallucinate and enter a dream state. Would it be a good dream or a bad dream, I wonder? There is some uncertainty in my recollection of this illness. I was terribly sick, and this very well may have been another near-death experience. I remember my mother crying and feeling as though I was floating. Could this mean that in one path of my life I died and in another, I lived? In other words, was this another example of a fork in the road of time? Am I still in a dream? Merrily, merrily, merrily, merrily, life is but a dream.

PLEIKU ON THE LINE

In April 1971, my brother Alf was stationed at Firebase 6, just southwest of Pleiku Airbase in the Central Highlands of South Vietnam. The primary mission of Pleiku Air Base was forward air controller missions coordinated with the South Vietnamese. It also served as a base for US Special Operations Forces (formerly called, *"Air Commando units"*) in the Central Highlands. It was a joint-service base operated by the U.S. Air Force with units from the Army, Navy, and Marines stationed there. My brother was a mobile radio operator and often worked with South Vietnamese Army (ARVN), and South Korean Marines (ROK Marines), in addition to our American forces. My brother wrote that he and the others at his air base in Pleiku were using an old artillery shell as a urinal and it was facing north, so they could piss towards Hanoi.

On April 21, 1971, Firebase 6 came under heavy rocket and mortar attack. Alf said that it was the most frightening experience he had in Vietnam. He didn't think he was going to survive. One rocket hit his jeep and destroyed it just a few minutes after he had stepped away to get something to eat. A close call. The day after this intense attack, two U.S. Air Force majors crashed their OV-10 Bronco on the runway. Alf had worked with one of them and was having difficulty dealing with their deaths. The most remarkable thing that happened during the attack was that my mom sensed what was going on. At around 2 o'clock in the morning on April 21, 1971, mom woke up screaming and crying. Dad was trying to comfort her. My room was right next to theirs, and I knew something terrible had happened. I entered mom and dad's bedroom and saw both sitting on the side of the bed.

"What's wrong mom?" I asked.

"Your mother had a bad dream," said dad.

"No! It wasn't a dream!" mom shouted.

"Olaug, it had to be a dream," dad said assuredly.

"No! I heard explosions, and then I heard Alf's voice. He said: 'Help mom, help.' Then I saw him standing here in his uniform in our bedroom; he was crying," she explained before she broke down and started crying softly. I had rarely seen my mother cry. My parents were not emotional people, at least not outwardly. I was worried; we were all worried. Was my brother okay? Had he been killed? These were worries shared by millions of American families during the Vietnam War.

One week later, my brother called home on a MARS line. We were so relieved that he was alive, mom was almost speechless. The Military Auxiliary Radio System (*MARS*) was a U.S. Department of Defense sponsored program, managed and operated by the US Army and the US Air Force. The program was a civilian auxiliary made up of licensed amateur radio operators who are interested in assisting the military with communications, especially with military families. My brother told my mother about how frightened he was the week before when Firebase 6 was attacked. Mom almost dropped the phone. The attack took place at approximately 5 o'clock in the afternoon in Pleiku, South Vietnam. That would be 2 o'clock in the morning in Seattle, and mom had somehow connected psychically to my brother at the same time he thought he was going to die and called out to her. I understand that this wasn't uncommon in the Vietnam War experience. How does it happen? No one knows.

THE TOUCH

In 1972, when I was 13 years old, my parents and I traveled to Norway. It was a sad occasion because my grandmother Mimmi had just died. The last time I had seen her was when I was four years old and her favorite grandchild. When we got up north to the island where my grandmother had lived, I noticed that her house looked great from the outside. Her flowers had started to bloom, and the place looked cheery. Once we stepped inside, I saw that everything looked like grandmother was still there. There was still food in the cupboards and all her knickknacks were arranged just as she always had them. I noticed that she had about ten bottles of ketchup in her cupboard, a delicacy my brother Alf and I had introduced to her in 1963. It was ironic that she had so much ketchup because she was horrified by our use of the stuff, calling it pig food. I slept in the room next to grandmother's room. All the bedrooms in her house had names. My grandmother's room was called the South Loft, my little room was called the Gable Loft, and my parent's room was called the Living Room Loft. The house felt a little bit eerie knowing that she had been alive only a few months before. My grandmother Mimmi had been the only grandparent that I had ever met.

One day, mom and dad went next door to visit our cousins. I was going to finish my Strat-o-Matic baseball game and follow after them. I climbed the steep stairs to my room and put the game away then came back down. As I turned away from the living room toward the kitchen, I felt kind of strange; my senses were tingling. Suddenly I felt a hand on my shoulder. I quickly turned around and found that no one was there, but I felt a presence, it was my grandmother Mimmi, I could even smell her familiar fragrance. I quickly put on my boots and ran out of the house and next door to tell my parents. The touch I felt was from my grandmother. I knew it was her. I had run so fast that I was out of breath when I stomped into our cousin's house, that lived down the street.

"I felt grandmother Mimmi touch my shoulder!" I said both breathlessly and excitedly. Everyone was quiet, then our cousin Øyvind spoke up.

"Oh yeah, that happens all the time around here," he said, then there were nervous smiles from mom and dad and my cousin's wife. People are very superstitious in Northern Norway. The island of Andøya is filled with spirits, thousands of years' worth of them. In between my grandmother, Mimmi's house and cousin Øyvind's house stood an old broken-down farm house. It belonged to my great uncle Oluf and his wife, Oldine. She was a Sami (sometimes called Lapplander) and was tiny. She was probably four and a half feet tall. It was said that she was very visually striking, and she took to my sister when my sister was a little girl before they moved to America. They were constant companions. After Oluf had died, Oldine lived in their old house by herself. When Øyvind built his home right next to her dilapidated home, she told him to never tear down her house, or she would come back to haunt him after she died. So, he was afraid and didn't tear down the house, in fact, he let that house eventually collapse in on itself.

One day, before my parents left for America, Oldine came out of her house and was choking. Dad was working outside and saw her struggling to breathe. He grabbed her ankles and held her upside down until the food came out of her throat. My dad was very strong. Oldine thanked my father and told him that she had a premonition that she would die by choking.

"Well, not this time," dad said as he smiled.

"Next time, you'll see," she said. And, sure enough, that's how she died. Whenever we visit the old house in Norway, I feel the presence of my ancestors. They never leave.

On the Mexican holiday, *Dia de los Muertos* (Day of the Dead), the people celebrate the lives of their ancestors. According to this Mexican cultural tradition, people die three deaths. The first death is when the heart stops, the brain ceases to function, and there is no respiration, a physical death. The second death is when the body is lowered into the ground and buried. The third death is when there is no one left alive to remember the deceased person—this is the final and most definitive death. I've seen the ghosts of both the recently departed and those who have no one left on earth to remember them. Perhaps we're all just gathering pieces of the same puzzle.

MEDIC!

The end of September 1973, I was coming home from school when I stopped at my friend, Chuck's house where some of the other neighborhood kids had gathered.

"Let's play some football," said Chuck.

"Yeah," said Ellery who had short dark hair and a stocky frame.

"Let's go over to Devon's house, he's got a bigger yard," said Chuck.

"Okay, but I don't know Devon," I said.

"He just moved into the neighborhood," said Chuck. The other kids were being quiet and not saying anything; I wondered why? Chuck was our organizer, especially when it came to sports. He had an odd physical deformity that other kids would tease him about, but not me. Chuck had a breastbone that stuck out quite a bit. "Come on guys, let's go play," said Chuck.

"I don't want to," said Ellery.

"Me neither," said another kid that I didn't know. Chuck just stared at them.

"His family is black," said Ellery, finally.

"So, what," said Chuck.

"I don't wanna hang out with black people," said Ellery.

"My dad said we should stay away from them," said another kid.

"Why?" I asked. Nobody answered. Devon was the only black kid on the block as it turned out. Then I could see that Chuck had come up with a solution like he always did.

"You guys are just chicken!" yelled Chuck.

"No, we ain't!" complained Ellery.

"Chicken, chicken, chicken!" screamed Chuck as he winked at me.

"Come on guys, let's play, we ain't chicken," commanded Ellery as all the other kids followed him to Devon's yard.

We gathered in Devon's yard, and soon Devon came out of his house, happy to see us.

"Cool, let's play," said Devon who was a slender boy. We started throwing the ball around, and then we discovered that we had an odd number of kids. It was then that Devon's dad came out of the house to check on us.

"Playing some football, boys?" he asked. Devon's dad wasn't tall, but he had an athletic build.

"Yes, sir," I said.

"Hey, can you play with us?" asked Chuck. Devon's dad thought for a moment, then joined us. He was a great player, and so was Devon. Chuck was our quarterback, of course, and I was the center. I was always on the line, in the trenches. I noticed that Devon's dad had a limp when he ran and walked.

"Why does your dad limp?" I asked Devon.

"He was in the war," said Devon.

"What war?" asked Ellery.

"Vietnam, you dumb shit," said Chuck. Ellery and Chuck squared off, ready to fight. Ellery snorted like a little bull when he was mad.

"Come on, boys, let's play," said Devon's dad who came between Ellery and Chuck. We had a great time and played for almost an hour. Then we decided to take a break and Devon's mom brought out some Kool-Aid for us to drink. She was a pretty lady, and nice.

"What did you do in the Army," I asked Devon's dad.

"I was in the Navy. I was a corpsman working with the Marines," he said.

"Corpsman, is that like a medic?" I asked.

"Yeah," said Devon's dad as he laughed.

"What's your name?" I asked.

"Lamont Johnson. And what's yours?"

"Bruce," I answered. "My brother was in Vietnam."

"How's he doing?" asked Mr. Johnson with a very concerned look.

"Okay, he's a little different than before he left," I answered.

"Yeah, I know," said Mr. Johnson with a sad look on his face.

"Is Vietnam where you hurt your leg," I asked.

"Yeah, got shot," he said. He showed us the scar, and we were all very impressed, even Ellery. We started playing again, and the game was going well until Mr. Johnson accidentally hit my forehead with his elbow. I began to bleed, a lot. Blood was pumping out of my head, and I was freaking out. The other kids were yelling and screaming.

"Medic! Medic! He's gonna die!" shouted Ellery. That's what we had heard on so many of the war movies we had all seen. Mr. Johnson tore off his t-shirt and applied pressure to my wound. Then, everything changed around me as if the world was in slow motion. I could see everyone and their expressions like I was floating above them and all around them. Their voices were muffled and slowed down. I saw a bright light above me along with an angelic face. Was it my guardian angel? Then everything came back at normal speed, and I felt as if I was punched in the gut and could hear everyone's voices in real time.

"I'm applying pressure," Mr. Johnson said. He turned to his son Devon.

"Get my medical bag, son!" he commanded. Devon ran into their house and brought back an olive-green bag with a red cross on the side. All the other kids gathered around me.

"He's a medic, you'll be okay," said one kid.

"Corpsman," I said. Mr. Johnson had me lie down on the grass and told the other boys to elevate my legs with some piles of leaves.

"You'll be okay son," he reassured me. Then he dressed and bandaged my wound and tied the bandage around my head to secure it. My head was covered with blood, and it was starting to crust up in my hair. The front of my shirt was covered in blood.

"Man, he lost a lot of blood," said Ellery.

"No, it just looks like a lot," said Mr. Johnson, "But it's a serious wound, and you'll need some stitches," he added. After a few minutes, I could get up.

"Where do you live?" asked Mr. Johnson.

"Not far," I said.

"I can drive you," said Mr. Johnson.

"No, that's okay, it's close," I said.

"I can walk with him," said Chuck. Mr. Johnson nodded his head.

"You sure you're okay?" he asked.

"Yeah," I said. The other kids had already lost interest in my wound and were playing catch. I saw that Mr. Johnson was upset.

"You okay?" Chuck asked Mr. Johnson.

"Yeah, okay," said Mr. Johnson.

"I've seen lots of blood," he added.

"Thank you, sir," I said as Chuck helped me up to make my way home. After walking a bit, I turned around and saw Mr. Johnson on his knees in the yard where I had bled onto the ground, holding the bloody t-shirt, and crying.

"Should we go back?" I asked Chuck.

"No, he'll be okay," said Chuck. I looked back again, and I could see Devon hugging his dad who was looking down and then up into the sky. The other kids had already found another yard to play their game.

When I got home, mom freaked out to see me covered in blood and with a head bandage. I told her what had happened.

"Chuck said I would have bled to death if it wasn't for Mr. Johnson," I told her.

"You were lucky he was a medic, he saved your life," she said as she hurried to get her coat and purse to take me to the doctor to get stitches.

"You have a guardian angel watching over you," she said. A guardian angel just like in Norway so many years ago, when my parents thought I had polio.

OPEN CASKET

When I was growing up in Seattle, my parents had many Norwegian-American friends. Almost all of them were unusual characters. One of my dad's best friends was named Asbjørn, Asbjørn Brandso. He used to work in Alaska with my dad in the 1950s. A carpenter by trade, this other Asbjørn was a highly skilled wood carver and artist. His wife Gudrun was quite an accomplished painter. They never had children, but often accompanied us on family vacations. He was a funny man and could make different animal noises that fooled people. One time we traveled to Canada with him and his wife Gudrun. Asbjørn Brandso bought a lot of Canadian whiskey and had it hidden in the trunk of his car on the way home. We stopped at the U.S. border, and the customs agent asked if he had anything to declare.

"No! What is this? Do you think I have a trunk full of Canadian whiskey or something?!" he asked the astonished customs official. They waved him through. Another time we were camping and the people next to our campsite had a little girl. Every time the girl walked past our campsite, Asbjørn Brandso would make a strange duck noise. The girl was fascinated and hurried back to tell her parents. She came back with her parents, and they were looking through the bushes for the baby duck she swore she had heard. Asbjørn was just sitting by the fire carving, and when they looked the other way, he would again make the duck noise. It was hilarious.

In February 1978, Asbjørn Brandso passed away. Mom and dad wanted me to go to the memorial. I think it was my first funeral and I was nervous. When we got to the funeral home in Ballard, Washington (where many Norwegians lived), there was a coffin situated in front of the mortuary chapel surrounded by flowers and a carving of a bald eagle that he had made. There he was, in an open casket. Dead. I was horrified. I hadn't been to a funeral, much less an open-casket funeral. I used to hang around graveyards when I was younger, and I even saw a dead boy who had drowned, but this was different. Now the dead person was someone I knew. Everyone took their turn marching past the coffin and paying their last respects. Gudrun, his widow, sat by herself in a crying room behind a thin black veiled curtain. I could hear her sobbing. It was heart-breaking. Overwhelmed, I was trying to take all of this in when I heard a voice.

"Don't be afraid," the voice said. It sounded like Asbjørn Brandso, but how could it be? He was dead. He was dead in a coffin right in the front of the chapel where I was sitting.

"Don't be afraid," the voice said again. Now I knew it was Asbjørn Brandso's voice. I could see his body in the coffin, and I didn't notice his body or his lips move. His face was sunken in, and he was pale and lifeless. There is a cold stillness to death that's hard to describe unless you have seen it firsthand. You can feel it.

"It will be okay, don't be afraid," he said in his distinctive Norwegian-American accent. I was starting to freak out but was eventually able to keep my cool. I wanted to say something to my mom, but I didn't.

"There is nothing to be afraid of," he said, "I'm okay." Then, the voice stopped,

I didn't hear anything else. I decided to walk up to the coffin and see him up close. He didn't speak to me again. I thought he was ancient, but he was only 68 years old when he died. As I type this, I'm 58 years old. Everything is relative. I can't explain how or why I heard his voice, but it was definitely his voice from beyond death.

HELL IS EMPTY

In the early spring of 1978, I moved into my brother Alf's garage. Mom and dad were in Norway for five months and had rented out our family home in Kenmore, Washington. I was nineteen years old and leaving for Alaska in six weeks, so living temporarily in my brother's garage didn't seem like a big deal. I slept on a mattress on the concrete floor in front of my rusty, oil-dripping, 1967 Triumph Spitfire. Alf was living by himself and didn't have a lot of food in the house. Since I didn't work or have any money, finding enough food to eat was a problem. When my girlfriend Marianne's mother got tired of me eating at their house, I scrounged pennies and nickels from the garage floor and from the coffee cans on the dusty shelves to buy a loaf of Wonder Bread.

Sometime later as I was walking home late one night through our neighborhood, I took a shortcut through a back alley. I walked past Old Lady Burns' house. She was the neighborhood witch. The legend was that many years earlier her husband had died at home, but she didn't report it to anyone. He sat rotting in a chair in the living room for a month or two until the neighbors complained of the smell emanating from the house. Since that time, her legend grew steadily. I was the only kid in the neighborhood brave enough to go trick or treating at her house. It didn't help to disprove her reputation that her property was overgrown with blackberries and weeds and that her house was unpainted and collapsing in around her. The only lights she used were kerosene or candles. Every kid on the block was afraid of her, and every adult was horrified by the thought that her old house brought down property values in the neighborhood. I looked into her side window as I walked past and saw the candlelight flickering. When I get nervous, I start whistling, and this time wasn't any different. She must have heard me whistle because she came to the window and stared at me. The old multi-paned window framed her pale, sickly face. Her wild, white hair shot off in all directions, and the sizeable cancerous ulcer on her nose seemed to pulsate. I wanted to look away, but I couldn't. I was frozen in her fixed stare, and my heart rate doubled. Then I ran. Fast.

A few days later, I was lying in my bed thinking about how I had mistreated Marianne that day. I had pushed her down, again. I was an asshole. Later in the day, we continued our argument, and I threw her car keys up on the roof of the garage. I seemed to be out of control. I was lying on my mattress bed, in the dark, on the concrete floor, when suddenly I felt a strange hot and tingling sensation in my feet. I peeked over my sleeping bag and saw a fire, cylindrical in shape, rising from the garage floor. Before I could react to the flames, it leaped up over my head in arc more than six feet in radius. I could feel the intense heat and pinched myself to make sure I wasn't dreaming. I was awake all right; I couldn't move except for the involuntary shaking, all I could do was watch. As the arc of fire raged above me in pulsating currents, I began to hear a deep voice. The voice boomed over me and seemed to follow the current of fire in the arc. I couldn't understand the words.

"Ah kum ra. Da he do, kam hin so la, Ikkuma tonrar dessssss," said the demonic voice over and over again.

After what may have been minutes or hours, the fire stopped. I fell into a deep sleep or passed out; I'm not sure which. I awoke the next day as the morning sunlight hit my eyes through the filthy, cobweb covered garage window. I was completely exhausted—emotionally and physically. I wasn't sure if I should tell anybody what happened. Was I crazy? I had to tell someone because I felt like I would go nuts if I didn't talk about the experience.

I went to Marianne's house and had breakfast. Her parents had gone to the beach rather early that day, so there wouldn't be any hassles. I told her about the arc of fire and the voice. She didn't believe me at first and thought I was joking. Then Marianne got a worried look on her face.

"Ahh, Bruce, maybe we should call a psychiatrist, what do you think?" she asked.

"Okay, but not if they are going to commit me or something," I answered. Marianne called several doctors, and she may have made an appointment, I can't remember. The more I thought about the experience, the more I wanted to forget it happened and not ever talk to anyone about it, not even to my girlfriend. Soon I would be in Alaska, I thought, and away from trouble like this. Running away had always been a viable solution for me. Unfortunately, it wouldn't be my last encounter with an evil presence. The world was a much scarier place than I had imagined. As Ariel said in Shakespeare's *The Tempest*, Act I, Scene 1: "Hell is empty, and all the devils are here."

THE MOUNTAIN NYMPH

Having returned from my unsuccessful adventure in Alaska, in June 1978, I was heading for the mountains with my friends Rick and Bill. It was a beautiful day for a hike. Our destination was a trailhead in the Cascade Mountains near *Salmon la Sac*, in Eastern Washington. Native Americans had created the first trails through the *Salmon la Sac* area, a waypoint for journeys into the higher mountains. There was a mining boom in the 1880s and 1890s when miners had found gold and silver. People began moving into the area, and a town named Galena City was planned at the confluence of Camp Creek and the *Cle Elum River*. The railroad project never materialized, and neither did the town.

We drove in Rick's rusty yellow Dodge Polara for an hour from the interstate 90 exit onto a forest service road that would take us to the trailhead. The terrain was rugged, and the switchback road was treacherous. We were able to ford a small creek that was perhaps two to four inches deep. Shortly after that, we heard a loud clanking sound beneath the car. Something had fallen off and was dragging on the rough gravel road. We stopped to investigate and found that the exhaust pipe had disconnected midway back and was catching on every bump and rock in the road. Since the Polara was so low to the ground, I couldn't get under to reach the pipe to fix or dislodge the damaged section. I told Rick to get in and back the car up to the edge of the road which had a very steep embankment that plunged down into the creek. Bill didn't think it was a good idea, but I was undeterred. I figured I could get at the troublesome tailpipe if the back of the car were hanging over the edge. Brilliant, I thought. Rick began backing.

"That's far enough Rick. I can get underneath now!" I yelled, but he didn't hear me.

"Rick, stop, stop Rick!" I yelled, but it was too late.

"Fuck!" Bill screamed as Rick backed off the edge of the roadway, sliding back down the embankment in the Polara. I could see him trying to brake wildly, but he finally came to rest against a giant Douglas Fir. The back end of the car was crushed. I clattered down the embankment to talk to him to see if he was okay, but he just sat there staring straight forward. Then, with a terrible whining and revving of the engine, he accelerated and turned the wheel hard to the left causing the car to skid sideways and away from the tree. He proceeded further down the embankment and ended up on a smaller dirt road that led back to the main forest road. Lucky indeed. He drove back and picked us up, and then we parked at the trailhead to begin the hike. The back end of the car was smashed in and the trunk was difficult to open and shut, but that old Polara was still drivable. It was after that strange and miraculous event that I began to feel a presence come over me. It was as if some unseen force was guiding and pushing me forward.

I must have had quite a stride because it took all Bill and Rick had to keep up with me. Our typical game was to hike as fast as we could to see who was manlier, and more of a hiker.

"Slow down, Bruce," said Rick.

"I need to rest, I don't feel like racing today," said Bill.

I was still feeling a bit off. I couldn't explain it, but it was as if something was taking over my thoughts and actions.

"Yeah, sure, sorry, I must have gotten carried away," I said. We decided to stop and rest for a bit. While Bill and Rick sat together, I stood by myself, withdrawn, and pensive.

"What's wrong with you, Bruce?" Bill asked.

"Yeah, you seem different," added Rick. I didn't respond. I felt a desperate need to keep pushing on and didn't rest or sit down.

We made it to our camp, five miles up. Rick and Bill consumed their freeze-dried lunches expediently as I sat and stared at the lake. I didn't eat and maintained a state of quiet concentration. We set up camp as the sun was going down. We had a small fire, and I was quiet and still withdrawn. I wasn't sure why. We all went to bed, and I crawled into my comfy sleeping bag hoping that I would feel more like myself after some rest. Instead, I had some disturbing dreams. I started to dream about a mini-shopping mall in Kenmore, Washington, my hometown, where there was this elephant ride in the front of the Wigwam store.

As I approached the elephant ride, I noticed this beautiful girl with dark brown hair and green eyes. She motioned seductively with her hands for me to come to her. I couldn't resist her and approached with every intention of doing whatever she wanted me to do. Then, I began yet another dream. In an instant, I was transported to an old rundown house—it seemed like old Mrs. Burns' house. A candle was lit on a table, and I sat on the floor. The room was murky, the candle the only light. The same beautiful girl now lay on the couch. She was staring into my soul; I could feel it. Her large luminous green eyes compelled me to come to her. Her smooth naked body and plump breasts were too much to resist. Her sensual body undulated, and she beckoned me with waves of a delicate hand. I was thoroughly ready to submit to this girl when Rick woke me up.

"What the fuck, Bruce?" Rick asked as Bill also stared at me.

"What is it?" I asked.

"You were moaning and writhing all around the tent like some homo," said Bill. I told them the dreams I had. As I thought about the dream, the darkened heavens opened up and it started to rain, and it rained hard.

"Did you copulate with this dream girl of yours?" asked Rick.

"I started to, but you woke me up, shithead," I said as I laughed.

"You started to, well, I'm afraid that's enough. We gotta get outta here," he said.

"What are you talking about?" asked Bill.

"He's given in to the Succubus, so we're all in danger here!" said Rick.

"Succubus?" asked Bill.

"The female version of the Incubus," answered Rick.

"Up here she would be in the form of a mountain nymph," he added. Not questioning Rick's authority on such matters, we hurriedly began packing our stuff at daybreak and the rain kept coming. We threw on our packs and headed back for the trailhead down the slippery, muddy trail. We got to Rick's old car and threw our packs in and headed down the mountain as the rain drenched us and the landscape.

We drove past the spot where he had driven off the embankment and headed down the steep grade to the creek. As we approached the creek, Rick applied the brakes, but the brakes only squealed like a steel-scraping banshee and the car didn't slow down. I could see the creek coming up, and it was no longer a shallow creek, but a raging river swollen by the torrential rain. Rick tried to stop, but the car raced ever faster.

"Oh, my God!" yelled Bill.

"We're not stopping for shit!" screamed Rick. I sat quietly, stunned, but my heart racing. We hit the flooded torrent with a giant splash and the car stalled in the middle of the river. The water was halfway up the doors. I panicked and opened the door on the passenger side. Water rushed in and quickly filled the car up to the top of the seats.

"Fuck! We're gonna drown!" yelled Bill.

"Hang on, we'll make it," said Rick.

"This is our fate," I said with quiet resignation.

"Shut the fuck up, Bruce," Bill said. The car began to drift down the river and came to rest on a sandbar. We were doomed. We were stuck in the middle of the raging river, it was still raining, and the car was half-filled with water. With a last desperate turn of the ignition, the car miraculously started again, and we could get traction on the sandbar. Further down the sandbar we were able to get out of the river and found a side road that led back to the main road.

"I believe this was a miracle," Rick said. I nodded in silent agreement while Bill was speechless.

Only a mile from the interstate we saw another obstacle. A giant Hemlock had fallen over the roadway. There was no way to pass.

"Great. Now what do we do?" asked Bill.

"It'll be okay, something will work out for us, I'm sure," I said.

"Shut up, Bruce, I'm thinking," said Rick who wasn't too happy with me and blamed me for all the mishaps. I tried sawing the giant tree with our little camp saw, but after 20 minutes of vigorous sawing, there was hardly any progress.

"Keep sawing genius, this is all your fault," said Rick.

"Come on, that's not fair," I complained as I began to feel more like myself.

"He's right Rick, blaming Bruce isn't helping us get home," said Bill. Just as we were ready to give up hope, we saw a white jeep approaching from the other direction. It pulled right up on the other side of the fallen tree. A man with shoulder-length dark hair and a beard jumped out of his jeep with a chainsaw. He proceeded to saw the tree in half and then wrapped a chain around the trunk of the tree. The chain was attached to a winch on the front bumper of his jeep.

"Thanks, man, you're a lifesaver," said Rick.

"No problem, all in a day's work," said the bearded man with a sardonic smile. He got back in his jeep and revved the engine, and then the winch began to pull the chain. The little bit of tree that was still together separated with a snap and we had a way out.

I looked more closely at the man with the beard; he looked like Jesus. More specifically, he looked like the Jesus statue from the *Abbey View Cemetery* I visited as a child. A sad-faced Jesus. We got back in the old Polara and drove past the two halves of the giant tree and then stopped.

"Thanks again," said Rick. The bearded man just smiled and waved as he put away his equipment. As we drove down the road toward the highway, I looked back through the rear window and was startled. The Jesus man in the jeep was gone. How could he have driven away that fast?

THAT OLD BLACK MAGIC

When I met Anna, my first wife, I was working as the CQ (charge of quarters) Runner at the 77th MP Detachment, Coleman Barracks, Mannheim, West Germany. She came into the company on a Friday night. An MP (military policeman) had driven her to our unit in his jeep. Anna had been first assigned to the regular Military Police Unit but was later reassigned in "a deal that involved furniture," as she later explained.

Anna swished into our building wearing a cream-colored halter top and bright orange hot pants. She had short, spiky blonde hair. As was usual, word got out in the barracks that a new female guard had come in, so everyone was hanging out of their doors gawking while I escorted her up to her room. The next day I made a deal with my roommate who was assigned to help Anna in-process and tour the prison. I offered to work a shift for him if he would let me help her to process into the unit. I remember wanting to protect her from the barracks wolves who were already on the hunt.

During the next few days, I did everything I could to get closer to Anna, but she kept acting elusive, and, she was going out with other guys, driving me crazy, but I wanted her, I needed her. One day I walked by the unit armory that was in the basement of our barracks. Smitty, who was the unit armorer, was sitting in his cage cleaning a shotgun. As I walked by his cage, he looked up at me.

"Ya know, I've got some advice for you, Solheim," he said.

I looked at him, surprised to hear him talk to me. He had never said anything to me in the four months that I had been working there.

"What is it," I said curiously.

"That girl you're after, it won't work out, you two ain't good for each other, there'll be nothing but trouble for you," he said as he stood up to get another weapon to clean. I thought about what he said. Why would he offer such advice? Smitty wasn't known for his sage advice on anything. What possessed him to say something to me? He didn't know me or owe me anything. Was it so obvious that Anna and I were bad for each other or did he have some special purpose, perhaps driven to deliver this message by some unseen force? I didn't take the advice of this armorer of amoré, and I continued my courtship and married Anna only three months later.

Some strange things happened during our courtship that I should have taken more notice of but didn't. When we first met, we shared ghost stories. I told Anna about my grandmother, and she told me that in the third grade she saw an old lady floating in mist coming down the stairs of their old house in Minneapolis. I expressed my interest in Wicca, and I was very eager to learn more. One evening, while talking in Anna's barracks room, my future bride lit a scary looking candle. The drippings from the candle looked like they had accumulated over centuries. Anna told me about a man she had met the last time she was in Europe. His name was Gruff. He had taught her magical spells.

"Really? Was he a magician?" I asked.

"No, silly, a wizard," she said.

I thought for a moment. "Are you a witch?" I asked.

"No, I'm psychic, and I know your secret," she said.

"What do you mean, secret? You might have one, but certainly not me," I said.

"There's an old woman who has put a curse on you," she said calmly.

My blood ran cold. Oh, my God, did she mean old Mrs. Burns? She was the neighborhood witch who I think put a curse on me.

"Tell me more, oh mystic one," I said in a mocking tone that masked my fear. Anna described Mrs. Burns' house–broken-down, no paint, candle lights–and then she described the old girl herself. Once I got spooked enough, I told her that we had better get something to eat before they closed the *schnell imbiss* (German snack stand). I refused to eat in the disgusting army mess hall after one of the cooks poured his aftershave into the lime Jello, and I saw another one picking his nose over the steam tables.

A few days later, it was apparent that one of the counselors at the prison had been taking an interest in Anna. We called him Counselor Laveigh because he was a psychologist at the prison, and he was a real whacko. Anna and I were in her room when there was a knock on her door. I opened the door, and in walked Counselor Laveigh. He swept past me and set up a black candle, some tarot cards and a few other oddities on the nightstand; then he began uttering an incantation. Anna seemed interested in what he was doing; I had reservations. After a few minutes of his foolish incantations, the glass dish holding the candle suddenly broke in two.

"You see! They're here!" he yelled.

"Who?" I asked.

"The spirits," he said. Anna was sitting down and watching the spectacle. I was growing weary of his fakery.

"OK, time to pack up your little witch toys and go," I said.

"Do not disrespect the spirits," he said with big moonbeam eyes.

"No disrespect, but time to leave," I said. Counselor Laveigh packed up his things and prepared to leave, but then he turned around, and said,

"You have to be careful to only practice white magic, don't be lured into doing black magic," he warned.

"Sure," said Anna.

"Come see what I've set up in my room," he said.

"I don't know," I said looking at Anna trying to signal to her that we shouldn't go with him.

"Sure, okay, I'm curious," said Anna as she darted away after Counselor Laveigh. I followed reluctantly. We got to his room on the second floor (Anna and all the other female guards were on the third floor) and walked in. His room was dark and filled with burning black candles. Counselor Laveigh had hung an upside down cross over his writing desk, and above that was a goat head inside of a pentagram.

"So, just what kind of magic do you do here?" I asked.

"Only white magic, maybe a little gray when necessary," he said as he giggled in an oddly girlish way. I looked at Anna who was horrified.

"We have to go!" Anna said as she grabbed my hand and tried to rush me out.

"Wait! Don't you want to meet him?" Counselor Laveigh asked as we started to bolt out of his room.

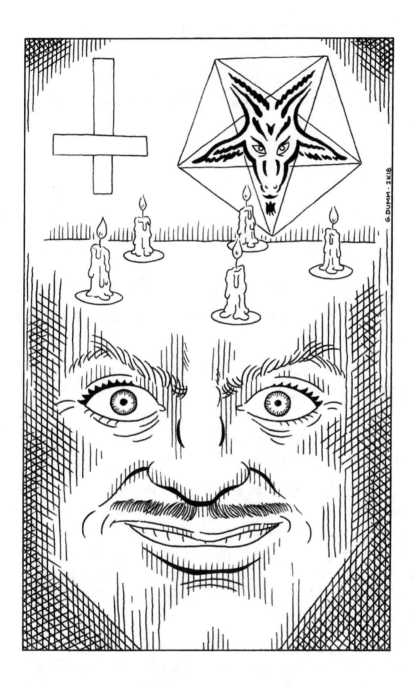

"No thanks, not really," Anna yelled back over her shoulder.

"Meet who?" I asked. She was dragging me along as we ran up to the third floor. We got into her room, and Anna locked the door.

"What the fuck was that?" I asked.

"Black magic," she said.

"Black magic?" I asked.

"The blackest!" she said. Anna's face reflected fear and trepidation.

"Can he do anything to us?" I asked.

"No, I don't think so," she said sheepishly. I paused to think for a moment.

"Maybe we need some kinda psychic defense...something more powerful than what he's doing," I suggested.

"Like what?" Anna asked. I wasn't sure, but I knew that I needed to go to the library to look up a few things.

The next day I was able to go to the library on post and found a book on demonology. Perfect, I thought. I can fight fire with fire. I checked out the book and went to the ceramics and pottery art studio that was in the recreation center. I showed the book to the instructor and told him that I was going to make a demon head. He then changed expression, looking more dangerous and odd.

"I've dabbled in demonology but had to stop because it was taking me to some dark places," he said with a weird look on his face (like two faces in the same face). I wasn't sure what he meant, but I started fashioning the head in spite of his comments.

It took me about an hour to make a demon head out of the clay, and it looked pretty scary.

"Oh, wow. That's exquisite," said the teacher on his return.

"Thanks, I like art, drawing, stuff like that," I said.

"I think I recognize this demon," he said as he began to thumb through my demonology book. He found something, then put the book down so suddenly that it fell off the table and the page he was on folded slightly.

"Ah, I have to go, other students need me, see you later," he said in a hurry as he left. I picked up my book and the demon head and started back to the barracks.

Anna wasn't in her room, but her roommate Riley let me in. Riley was very flirty, as usual, until she saw the demon head.

"What the hell is that thing?" she asked.

"A demon head, not sure which demon though," I said as I tried to find the page the ceramics instructor was on when he suddenly had to leave.

"I hope you're not going to leave it in here," Riley said.

"Nah, I just want to show it to Anna," I said. Riley hugged me and left the room. I put the demon head on the nightstand in front of a three-part mirror. I thought it would be cool to light a candle by the demon head and surprise Anna when she came back. After I had lit the candle, I lay down on the rug near Anna's bed. Then, suddenly, I thought I saw something move on the nightstand. I got up and looked more closely. The demon head had moved slightly to the side. I centered it again, and then I saw its lips move. I rubbed my eyes and pinched myself. Was I dreaming? No. The lips moved again, but this time it spoke.

"Fuck, fuck, fuck," it said. I sat and stared at it until its lips stopped moving and it was silent. The candle had burned itself out by that time. Then, Anna came in.

"Hey, what are you doing here?" she asked.

"Riley let me in," I said. Anna paused to look at me.

"Did she try to fuck you?" Anna asked.

"No, she left pretty quick," I answered. Then Anna saw the demon head.

"What the hell!" she yelled.

"I made it to ward off Counselor Laveigh and his black magic," I said.

"Get it out of here," she screamed.

"Why?" I asked.

"It's evil!" she said.

"I don't know about that, but its lips moved, and it talked," I explained.

"Yeah, exactly! Because it's evil!" she screamed. Then she noticed the demonology book. Anna picked up the book and read the page that was folded when the ceramics teacher dropped the book down and left in such a hurry.

"Asmodeus, God of Lust, and there are minor demons associated with him," she read.

"Get that fucking thing out of here, now!" Anna demanded.

"But it took me a long time to make it," I complained. Anna then grabbed the demon head and rushed to the window that was slightly open. The big dumpster stood below her window. She hurled the demon head out of the window, and it landed with a thud in the dumpster. I was sad, but I was glad too. The thing was starting to scare me.

"I made the same demon head in 9th grade," said Anna who was in shock.

"The same? Are you sure?" I asked.

"Yeah. We're linked in some strange way. I destroyed mine, and I had to destroy yours. You were starting to connect with that thing," she said. I was speechless. Anna and I both had psychic powers, and together we seem to attract paranormal phenomena, like a magnet. We had to be more careful. Lesson learned: don't mess around with things and forces you don't understand.

THE HILLS ARE ALIVE

Because we were stationed in Germany while Anna and I were in the army, we got to visit her relatives in Austria quite often. I'll never forget the first time we visited her aunt in Bartholomäberg, Western Austria. Anna's mom was Austrian, and her father was Ukrainian. They met after World War II. Her father had been a prisoner in a Nazi concentration camp. Her aunt's house was nestled on a steep mountainside in the Austrian Alps. It was truly the *Sound of Music* comes to life. Beautiful and inspirational. Her aunt's house was a typical mountain home with whitewashed walls and exposed brown timber framing and trim. Our room was on the second floor with an antique bed and a wardrobe cabinet (*schrank* in German). The windows in our room looked out across the valley to the mountains on the other side.

I fell into a deep sleep that night under the feather blankets, breathing the cool, clean, mountain air. We were sleeping in Anna's grandmother's room that included her furniture. Anna's grandmother had a tough life. Her husband was a Nazi party official who had abandoned her and their children and had taken up with a neighbor lady; he eventually had a child with her. That child was mentally disabled and rarely left the house. Ultimately the grandfather wanted to move his mistress and their child into the home where Anna's grandmother lived. The grandmother wouldn't stand for it, but he insisted and had her committed to an insane asylum to get rid of her. While Anna's grandmother was in the mental institution, Nazi doctors gave her shock treatments, chained her up, and gave her combinations of powerful drugs that damaged her mind, soul, and body. After the war, she was released, and the grandfather was arrested. Anna's

65

grandmother lived with Anna's aunt for the rest of her life, she never recovered and had gone quite mad.

So, there we were, sleeping in her room, surrounded by her antique furniture. In the middle of the night, I woke up because I felt a strange sensation. I opened my eyes, and I saw a person in the corner of the room, by the wardrobe and the windows. I was startled, I thought that maybe Anna's aunt had come into our room to tell us something, but it wasn't Anna's aunt. This person was an older woman, and she wasn't quite all there, meaning that she was translucent, a ghost. There was a ghost in our room! I woke Anna up and had her confirm that she saw the ghost too. The apparition was just floating there, in the room, by the window, staring at us. She had white hair, pulled back in a bun, dark clothing, and was staring directly at me.

"I just want to make sure I'm not imagining this…you see what I see?" I asked Anna.

"Yes, I do," said Anna, as I pinched myself and made sure I was awake.

"And we're not dreaming, right?" I asked.

"Not dreaming," Anna said.

"Who is she?" I asked.

"My grandmother," she said.

"Are you sure?" I asked.

"Yes," Anna said.

We watched her grandmother's ghost for a while, utterly terrified, and then she vanished. Somehow, we got back to sleep. We woke up early the next day.

When Anna and I came downstairs, her aunt was already up and making breakfast.

"Good morning," she chirped.

"Good morning," I said.

"We saw grandma last night," Anna blurted out. Her aunt smiled, un-phased.

"Yes, we all do, dear," she said. Anna and I looked at each other, astonished.

"Why didn't you tell us about her?" Anna asked. Her aunt put a dish in front of each of us with eggs and toast.

"We figured you knew," she said.

We finished our breakfast and later that day we visited the local Catholic Church. It was a beautiful old church with an exquisitely painted altar. The priest was there and greeted us.

"Hello," he said, "I've heard you're visiting from America?" he asked.

"Stationed in Mannheim, US Army," I said in German.

"And you speak German, excellent," he said with a smile. He gave us a tour of the church and graveyard on the church grounds. Some of the graves were 200 years old.

"Do you know anything about ghosts?" I asked as Anna poked me in the ribs.

"Well, sure, departed spirits…why do you ask?" he asked.

"We saw Anna's grandmother last night in the house," I said. The priest thought for a moment, perhaps trying to choose just the right words.

"If you know the story of Anna's grandmother, then you know she was a tortured soul," he said.

"Yes, we know the story," I said.

"She does haunt this area, mostly the house where she lived, but also other places, the church as well," he said.

"You've seen her?" I asked.

"Oh yes, and many others," he said. We walked around the church grounds a bit more, and then he bid us farewell. Apparently, people in that mountain village accepted ghosts as a matter of routine. Perhaps living, as most of us do, suffering from historical amnesia in a modern, busy, transient world, we don't notice the ghosts among us. However, in these quiet, tucked away, old places, it's easier to encounter those that have passed on. Perhaps there are fewer distractions in such places. Seeing the grandma ghost was one of the most intense paranormal experiences I've ever had.

NOT SO GOOD VIBRATIONS

After Anna and I got married in Copenhagen, Denmark, in 1979, we left the army barracks and moved into an apartment approximately one kilometer away from Coleman Barracks. We didn't know that an unfurnished apartment in Germany was more austere than in America. We rented our apartment above a gasthaus (like an inn with bar and grill and rooms to rent). There were no appliances, no cabinets in the kitchen, even some of the light fixtures were missing. This apartment was located at 52 Memeler Strasse in Mannheim. Every night we heard the jukebox playing loudly and people drinking, trying to talk over the music. Pink Floyd's *Just another Brick in the Wall* played day and night. On Thursday nights, the old German war veterans would gather for their meeting wearing green uniforms. They would gobble down dozens of schnitzels, drink beer, and schunkel (join arms and sway to and fro) to old German songs. As the evening wore on, and after more beer and shots of Jägermeister, the songs they were singing started to sound like old Nazi songs from World War II.

The landlady, Frau Schultz, was a complete bitch, and so was her fat-faced son. I nicknamed him Triple F (Fat Face Fucker). I think we were paying for more than our share of the electricity. One day the landlady was vacuuming in the hall and stairway upstairs on the same floor as our apartment. Suddenly the vacuuming stopped, and our power went out. When the power came back on, the vacuuming continued. I complained, but she denied it. Another time I got locked out of our apartment and had to climb the balcony to get in. Triple F saw me and reported this to his mother who then called the US Army housing office and filed a complaint against me. After I had explained about the electricity and other things she was doing, the army clerk in the housing office told me that our landlady was a real problem for them. She kept renting to GIs, and the same thing happened every time—She took their large deposit, overcharged them on rent, and eventually kicked them out.

The first few months we had to sleep on the floor and cook our food in an electric skillet. Despite the spartan conditions and the evil landlady, it was still better than living in the barracks. There was a grassy common area behind our gasthaus apartment building and beyond that, several other apartment buildings. One night I was having trouble sleeping because of my allergies. There was a linden tree just outside of our apartment, and the pollen was making me sick. I had never in my life had such severe allergies. Twice I had to go to the emergency room for breathing problems. So, I was half awake when I felt a tug on my foot like someone was trying to pull me off the bed. I had this horrible feeling that something was in the room, but I saw nothing. I woke up Anna, but by the time she was awake, the sensation had passed. It was terrifying. I got up to get a drink of water, and then I returned to the bedroom and looked out of our back window and noticed lights were on in a few of the apartments in the buildings on the other side of the green space. In one of the apartment windows that was dimly lit, I saw a dark shadowy figure, just standing there, watching me. Perhaps he saw me looking and quickly moved away from the window, in a most unnatural way. It looked like he was hovering or floating. I got an immediate chill from the creepiness of it all, and then I reluctantly went back to bed.

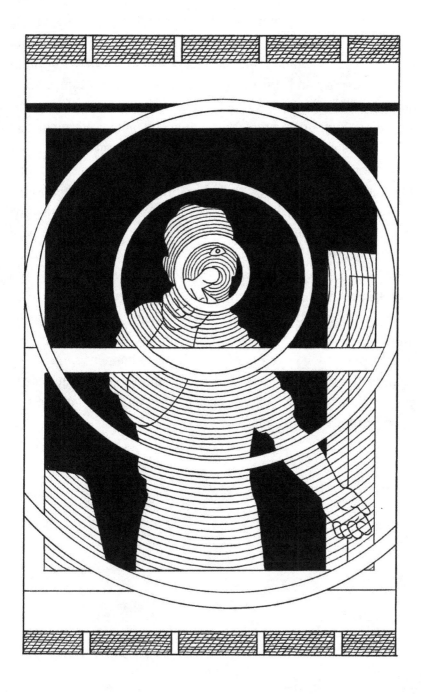

A few nights later, I awoke to everything vibrating on the little table we had by the bed. I thought it was an earthquake, but it wasn't. The vibration was only on the night table. Our alarm clock, Anna's hand mirror, and some other small things were moving with the vibration and some fell off the table. It was terrifying. I got up and ran around to check on everything else in the apartment. All was fine, but the vibration continued. Then I looked out our bedroom window over the green space at that apartment building where I had seen the mysterious shadow figure. I was startled and took a step back. There was the shadow figure again, in the same apartment window, staring at me with his arms raised. Then he lowered his arms, and the vibration stopped. He then moved away from his window and disappeared into the darkness of his apartment as the lights were turned off. I stood and stared for a while in shock. Who was he? Why was he doing these things to us? How was he doing these things to us? I still don't know who, why, or how. It never happened again, but then, not long after, we moved. I suppose evil requires no explanation. Anna later told me that she felt that someone had been murdered in that apartment.

THOUGHT LOG

After my eldest son Bjørn was born in June 1980, we finally moved into a rental house instead of an apartment, it was on the bottom floor of a large family home. Our landlord lived upstairs and was an artistic blacksmith. The woods above the house we rented in Germany were called the Odenwald or Odin's Woods. Ober-Mumbach, the little village where we lived, was situated in the steep hills above and in between Weinheim and Heidelberg. There were old ruins around the hillsides that were said to have been built by the Romans. Witches were supposed to hold candlelight masses there, according to local legends. Ancient and spooky, the German countryside and hills exuded mystery. It was an incredibly picturesque and magical place to live. My army friends all lived in the depressing old Nazi army barracks. I would invite them to come over, and we would take walks through the woods. I would then tell them scary stories, something to ponder in dreams, but we would have a splendid time.

One day, after a few too many German beers, my friends and I decided to go for a hike and ambush some Germans. It was just for fun, of course, nothing serious, we just wanted to scare them a little. Luckily, no Germans came by that day. We sat there in the woods and as the sun sank lower, the trees began to put on their shadowy evening disguises. The leaves of fall lay all around. A fog began to settle in as we dozed lazily on pungent and musty smelling mossy logs and piles of leaves.

It was then that she appeared, a woman from the dense woods through the mist riding a gleaming white horse, her long wavy golden hair, highlighted by the setting sun, fell to either side of her rosy cheeks. With her luminous blue eyes, this beautiful Aryan Goddess stared at us.

"Oh, my God," said my friend Robert.

"Wow," I said. The others were speechless. The Goddess rode by us, and all seemed as if it were in a dream, in slow motion. She stared as she rode by, winking and tossing her hair back. Then, as suddenly as she had appeared, she galloped away, time sped up, and she was gone.

"This *is* an enchanted forest," I said.

"I've heard you say that before, I thought you were bullshitting, but now I believe it," said Robert who was mesmerized by the experience. Then all my other Army buddies chimed in.

"Me too," said Greg.

"She was the most beautiful woman I've ever seen," said Robert.

"A goddess," said Greg.

"Anyone want another beer?" asked Martinez. We all looked at him.

"This beautiful forest goddess mysteriously rides past us like some erotic fantasy dream, and all you can say is does anyone want a beer?" I asked.

"Well, I thought if we drank more, maybe we'd see her again," said Martinez.

"Good thinking," said Greg with a chuckle. We all consumed more German beer and headed toward the sportsplatz (a local athletic field). The lights were on, but no one was on the field. It was eerily quiet except for the sounds of our drunken stumbling. The fog had settled around the edges of the field and framed it like the shoebox displays filled with cotton balls that we made in grade school. We cautiously stepped out onto the field. Just then a bell rang out in the spooky fog with ear-splitting strength. Taking the bell ringing as a bad omen, we all ran down the trail toward my house.

The next day I went up to the same spot in the forest where we saw the Aryan Goddess and found a rather unusual log. Yes, it was the same one we had sat on before, but this time I examined it more carefully. I sat on the well-worn moss-covered wood. The gnarled branches were broken off and lay beside it. The roots were exposed on one end, it had an ancient, earthy smell, the treetop had snapped and lie decaying further from the main trunk. I sat and thought. The log seemed to stimulate my thinking. I could think clearly with no disturbing annoyances. It was the perfect place to relax and think—a zone of quiet peace with a mysterious aura. I named it the "thought log." As I sat, I drifted off to sleep. In my ensuing dream, the Aryan Goddess reappeared. This time she dismounted her horse and walked gently towards me. I couldn't move even though I wanted to. She began to remove her silky white dress, but then the vision was interrupted, '*Brumm bump bump.*' the sound of a German marching band woke me up. There in front of me, marching up the trail, was a folk march group with a band. Weird and surreal. They were all decked out in traditional costumes, Lederhosen (leather shorts with suspenders), knee socks, and three-cornered hats with feathers. I nodded hello as they passed.

I returned to the thought log many times and found it to be a stimulating place to write and paint, but I never again saw the Aryan Goddess. I did, however, see lots of German marching bands and folk marchers during the rest of my time in Germany.

About one week later, after the Aryan Goddess incident, my wife Anna asked me: "Did your friend die in a plane crash?"

I was surprised she would ask that. "No," I said. Later I found out from my best friend Bill in Seattle that his sister had died in a small plane crash in Washington State. Then, in May 1980, Anna told me that Mt. St. Helens was going to blow up and that I should warn my family in Washington. Sure enough, on May 18, 1980, the mountain blew up. Anna and I seemed to be magnets for strange paranormal phenomena and being in Germany seemed to amplify and stimulate these strange occurrences.

KILL TANKS!

I was happy to leave the army and the military prison behind in 1981, but the happiness didn't last long. I couldn't find a decent job in the high unemployment ravaged economy of 1982 America. I tried to go to engineering school and failed miserably. The depression I was experiencing only worsened, along with my temper. Desperate for money, I joined the army reserves. The only problem was that the reserves didn't provide the income and benefits my family needed. I then went back to work in corrections. I worked for three months at the Oak Park Heights Maximum Security State Prison in Stillwater, Minnesota. It was awful, chaotic, and extremely dangerous. I wasn't there very long when I decided to quit and on my last night; there was a fire in segregation, we had to drag unconscious prisoners out of their cells. One prisoner came to and punched the guard that had just saved his life. It didn't make any sense. The air was thick with black smoke and I coughed up black phlegm for a month after. As much as I disliked being in the army, I missed the security, the routine, and the structure. The civilian world was frightening to me. While I was working in the state prison, I applied for U.S. Army Warrant Officer Flight Training. My goal was to become a medical evacuation pilot (medevac). My brother had told me stories about brave young helicopter pilots in Vietnam rescuing injured soldiers. I had to convince Anna, that it was the right thing to do.

"I'll be an officer. It'll be different. I don't want to hurt anyone; I want to help people, so being a Medevac Pilot is the perfect solution," I said.

"Uh huh," she said, unconvinced.

Before I started flight school, I began to have recurring nightmares. One of the nightmares would start with me on the ground somewhere in what appeared to be a tropical environment. Small children surrounded me in torn and ragged clothing. Boom! Boom! Boom! Explosions and fire all around us. The Cobra attack helicopters were coming. They were attacking the children and me. I grabbed two babies and had the other children follow me as we ran toward some thatched huts that stood on stilts. The Cobra gunships swooped in again and began firing rockets with flechette rounds (small razor-like projectiles). We reached the huts and entered just as the flechettes ripped through the walls. Everything caught on fire. The children and I were shredded—death was everywhere, and I began screaming. That's the point at which I'd wake up. In another recurring nightmare, I'd be flying in a helicopter by myself. A blinding flash and a fiery explosion destroyed the aircraft around me, and I was left by myself flying through the air without the helicopter. I always woke up before I hit the ground. Despite the nightmares, I kept going. Our Training, Advising, and Counseling (TAC) Officer continually reminded us of what would happen if we quit or failed.

"Go ahead and quit candidate. We have the paperwork all ready for you in the office along with coffee and donuts. No more abuse, no more training, you'll be all set. Then we'll ship you off to cook school. The army needs good cooks," he said. Or I could end up back in corrections. I couldn't quit.

About two-thirds of the way through flight school, the day came for us to be assigned our transition aircraft. The type of helicopter we would fly would determine our job. I wanted to fly the UH-1 Huey, the helicopter used for medical evacuation. Our Senior TAC Officer (who later would lose his job for fraternization with warrant officer candidate wives) announced the assignments.

G. DUMM · 2K18

"Warrant Officer Candidate Solheim, OH-58, Aeroscouts," he said. No, that couldn't be right, I thought. I wanted to be a medevac pilot. Now the army was going to train me for combat as an aerial scout. I was devastated. The nightmares continued and intensified when I was assigned to Ft. Bragg, North Carolina. In 1984, I joined the Combat Aviation Battalion, 82nd Airborne Division. Our motto at the Combat Aviation Battalion was 'Kill Tanks.' Every time our unit would gather, the commander would have us jump to our feet and shout the unit motto at the top of our lungs. After a few months in my unit, my misplacement in a combat role was jeopardizing my flying career. I began to have doubts about my being in the Army and being a pilot. I was taking college courses at night, and my interests seemed to be far from the flight line. The war training and the mindless mottos began to wear on me. I started asking forbidden questions of those around me. One day, the commander came into the briefing room, and everyone jumped to their feet to yell the motto.

"Kill tanks, sir!" they said. I remained silent, and then I turned to my friend Darrell.

"Shouldn't we say, kill people in tanks, isn't that what we're really doing?" I asked.

"Shut up, Bruce," he said.

"I mean, think about it, tanks are inanimate objects," I added.

"You think too much," he said.

"It just seems stupid to not acknowledge what we're really doing," I said.

"You know what? You don't belong here. You're like an artist in a room full of engineers," he said.

Darrell was right. I thought too much, and I didn't fit in. My old stick buddy was looking out for me. I had to listen to him. I also thought about how my marriage was falling apart. I knew I was miserable to be around, maybe that was it. I was moody, angry, sensitive, and not fun.

The nightmares continued, and I began to feel unsafe flying. Around that time, we started to receive secret briefings about a planned invasion of Nicaragua. We were on constant alert, and a few times we were called in, locked up and held on base with full combat gear, helicopters loaded, ready to go to war. We stood at the precipice, and I was staring into the abyss. I tried to ask my commander for a transfer to a medevac unit, but it was declined. I didn't want to kill anybody. My mission would lead me to kill someone; I knew that. And that day was coming soon. I decided that I needed to share my anger, sadness, fears, and doubts with our chaplain.

"How can I deal with the fact that my mission would eventually lead me to kill someone?" I asked thinking that he wouldn't have a convenient answer for that question. The chaplain patted me on the back and gave me a sideways hug.

"My son, remember, you'd be killing Godless communists," he said. It was at that point that I knew I had to get out of the military. My nightmares were a sign. I wasn't in the right place or doing the right thing, at least not for who I wanted to be. I was meant to do something else.

THE TWIN ANGELS

In 1986, I bought my first house. It was built in 1924 and was located on East Marine View Drive in Everett, Washington. The price was $52,000. Our home was close to the Everett Pulp Mill, and on certain days the rotten egg sulfur smell was bad enough to make you throw up. We had a daylight basement and two stories. Bjørn and Byron, my two eldest sons who were born in Germany, shared a bedroom on the Northside of the house upstairs. In the living room and dining room we had an excellent view of the Cascade Mountain Range and Mt. Pilchuck. We painted that old house and fixed up the basement as a recreation room and made it into a comfortable family home.

Our house wasn't in a great school district, in fact, my sons had to walk through the projects and by the juvenile detention center to get to Hawthorne Elementary school. On the Westside of Broadway Avenue (the main thoroughfare), was Whittier Elementary. The difference between the two schools was like night and day even though they were both public schools. Hawthorne was covered in graffiti, and most of the project kids went there. Whittier was in an affluent neighborhood, they had beautiful campus buildings and well-manicured grounds. One day, Bjørn and Byron brought home a blood-filled drug needle they found on the school playground. Many of their classmates were Cambodian refugees who kept chickens in their project apartments. There was an abandoned lot that stood between our house and the projects. The neighbor house to the north of us was owned by an old lady who lived alone. The neighbors to the south were a lovely old couple named Ray and Elsie. Ray had been a bomber pilot in World War II.

One night Bjørn and Byron woke us up suddenly.

"Daddy, there are angels in our room!" said Bjørn.

"What?" I said.

"Dad, mom, two little girl angels were in our room. They came in through the window," explained Byron.

"Oh, my God!" said Anna. I rushed into the boys' room to investigate.

"I don't see anything," I said.

"They came from over there, through our window," said Bjørn.

"Yeah, really, they did," Byron added. I looked through the window and saw the old neighbor lady's house. There was a light on downstairs, but no light upstairs. The upstairs window was directly across from the boys' bedroom window.

"You ever notice how there's never light on over there?" I asked.

"You're right," said Anna.

"We want to sleep in your room tonight," said Byron.

"Yeah," said Bjørn. The boys piled into the bed, and I switched off the light taking one last look at the neighbor's house.

A few days later I was cutting the lawn and saw Ray, our World War II Veteran neighbor.

"Hey Ray, is it just the old lady that lives on the other side of us in that big house?" I asked.

"Yeah, that old bird, she lives alone," he answered.

"You ever notice that there are no lights on upstairs, in the window?" I asked.

"She had it closed off," he said.

"Closed off?" I asked. Ray continued with his yardwork for a little bit while I looked dumbfounded.

"Yeah, she had sisters who were twins, their room was upstairs. They died of Scarlet Fever during the depression," he said.

An icy shudder ran down my spine, and the hairs stood up on the back of my neck. "Really?" I asked.

"After the twin girls had died, they boarded up the second floor of the house and closed it off," he said.

"So, the twins were little girls when they died?" I asked.

"Yeah," said Ray. I thought for a moment. Should I tell Ray that Bjørn and Byron saw the ghosts of those twin girls? I decided not to say anything.

A few weeks later, Anna met the old lady who lived in the ghost twin house. She was very nice and gave Anna some day-old bread and bakery goods.

"She works at the bakery still, at her age," said Anna.

"Ask her if we can come over," I said.

"What? Why?" asked Anna.

"I wanna take a look at the inside of that house," I explained.

"You mean you wanna find out about those ghosts, right?" she asked. I nodded yes. The next day we visited the old lady. She lived on the first floor and had antique furniture with black and white pictures hanging on the wall. While the old lady was in the kitchen, I examined the walls and ceiling. I could see where the access to the upper part of the house was closed off. The staircase had been removed. After we had returned home, I got my binoculars and peeked through the second-floor window of the old lady's house from the boys' bedroom window.

"Wow, that's creepy," I said.

"What?" asked Anna.

"There's old furniture and two little beds in that room," I said.

"Let me see," said Anna. Sure enough, the room was set up like it was from the 1930s. I talked to Ray, and he confirmed that they had left it just the way it was after the twins died in 1932.

A year later, the vacant lot behind our cozy old home was sold, and they started building three-story apartments. The neighborhood changed. The apartments that loomed over us and were filled with low-rent tenants who stared down at us, making rude comments and throwing beer bottles in our yard. There was constant noise from their blasting stereos, so, I decided that we had to move. I was accepted to a history doctoral program at Bowling Green State University, consequently, we sold our home in 1989 and moved to Ohio. The lady who bought our house reported to us a few months later that there were spirits, in the house, and that it was haunted. She thought we had left our spirits behind as a place memory, endlessly replaying like a tape loop, over and over again. Maybe, I didn't tell her about the twin girl angels.

Many years later I drove by our old house. The years had slid past faster than I could have ever imagined. The tree that my boys climbed was still there. The yard was grown over with weeds, and the garden fence and shack teetered on the brink of collapse. Paint peels dropped in long, curled shards from the side of the once bright yellow two-story family home. Someone had spray-painted ugly and unfamiliar gang symbols on the back wall. The carport had fallen in upon itself. The house had a poor folk's rental feel to it. Who lived in my old house? My family that lived there was no more. We had disintegrated and broken off in different directions. Our hopes and dreams were being buried beneath the years of neglect. The distant echoes of my children laughing in the yard were now drowned out by loud gangsta rap and death metal music emanating from the already dingy and broken down low-rent apartments looming in back. Our garden had grown over with weeds of discontent and loneliness. I sat there, in my car, gently sobbing, staring into the past. My tears over the loss of my old family home ran into a sea of tears from millions of other broken American family homes. Then, the broken-down car parked in front of me moved a little from side to side. Someone was sleeping inside of that car. What more proof did I need? This old neighborhood was dying. A transient and desperate new group of people squat on the ruins of a once proud middle-class section of town. My old house was still breathing, but barely. They say you can never go back; it's very true. My problem, however, is that I have trouble moving forward. In a strange way, I feel like those twin angels—forever locked up in the past.

GOLDEN MOM

My mother only had a sixth-grade education, but she didn't let that define or hinder her. She was very smart. She had a rare combination of practical folk wisdom, compassion, artistic talent, intuition, and a highly developed sixth sense. She was a great mom. That isn't to say that we didn't have our clashes, we did. I can still remember the only time I ever talked back to my mother, I did so ending my tirade with a flippant remark.

"Fuck you!" I said. I turned around after I said it and thought I had gotten away with something. The next thing I knew she kicked me in the butt so hard from behind that it raised me several inches up from the floor, I hit my head on the light fixture in the low ceiling in our downstairs hallway. Hers was a stealthy attack. I was in shock. I deserved it, of course, and I deeply regret what I said all these years later.

My mother was diagnosed with colon cancer in April 1990. I was finishing up my first semester of my doctoral program. I went back to Seattle to visit her in the hospital. Before I went back to Ohio, I helped bring mom home to die in her own house. She needed to be transported by ambulance because she was in such a weakened condition, so I drove separately. I arrived first, before mom, my brother or my dad, I noticed a large bird on the front porch of my parent's home. It was a raven. Birds are considered the harbinger of death in many cultures. We got her as comfortable as possible, and I then had to go back to Ohio for finals week. The night before she died I called her.

"You're the best mom in the world, and I love you," I told her. She laughed.

"Thank you," she said. It wasn't customary for my parents to say that they loved anyone, even me, but I knew she did. The next morning, May 4th, mom passed away, I experienced unimaginable grief. I felt lost and disoriented. I don't think that I can adequately describe how it felt or could have possibly anticipated how I would feel. Christmas time since her death has never been the same. Mom was Christmas to me. There were no more Norwegian cookies, food, and traditions. That was all her. After many years of being depressed about mom's passing, I started doing Norwegian Christmas myself. Now, I'm the keeper of the traditions.

Mom has visited me a few times since she passed away. One day after she died, I had just finished giving a final; the students had left, when I saw my mother in the doorway. It was a vivid vision. Mom was golden, even to the point of glowing gold. She seemed happy and was smiling as she stood in the doorway but didn't enter the classroom. She was no longer sick with cancer. She looked at me and smiled.

"There is a heaven," she said. That was it. She turned and left. I didn't even have time to ask her anything. She had delivered the message. Since that time, I've felt her presence in Norway. Both mom and dad. Our house in Norway is a hub for spirit visits. I've had many paranormal experiences but none with so much personal meaning as meeting my golden mother in my classroom. I didn't have a chance to ask her where Heaven is, I assumed that it's not on Earth, but I don't know for sure. I didn't ask her if she was in Heaven, I just assumed she was. Having had such experiences with people who have died, I didn't need to ask if there was life after death. All this has led me to believe that there is no death, at least not the way many imagine it to be. How do you get to Heaven? Well, that's another matter. I know it exists because mom told me it did exist and I believe her. The question is: Will I go there after I leave this world? Another, equally important question is: where would I go if I don't go to Heaven? We shall see.

NAMELESS

My life lessons kept coming in the early 1990s; each one seemed harder than the last. In February 1991, I was falsely accused and arrested for domestic violence. Leading up to this arrest, Anna and I had fought quite a bit as the strain of graduate school intensified our arguments. Earlier in our relationship I had been emotionally abusive and prone to outbursts of anger. Although the incident for which I was arrested didn't happen, I had been abusive in the past, so I can't say I was totally surprised that Anna called the police and for all intents and purposes ended our relationship. I knew it was my fault. I was arrogant and ignorant. I wasn't faithful and naively pretended that it didn't matter. It did matter, and I lost custody of my two boys and was out on the street before I knew it. Missing my boys, adrift, and emotionally numb, I began a series of relationships with women hoping that I would find happiness. I was careless and then one of my girlfriends became pregnant. My sense of responsibility clashed with my conscience. One weak and unthinking moment would change the rest of my life, and that of two other human beings. My girlfriend wanted an abortion. I was totally against it, but I was trying hard not to be manipulative. I shared my dilemma with my domestic violence class (court ordered), but I found no real support, only sharp opinions. I would pay for this I thought. My girlfriend told me that she was worried her decision would affect our relationship. I told her that I couldn't make any promises.

I agreed to take her to the abortion clinic. She didn't want me to go at first, but she didn't want to go alone, there was no one else to go with her since she couldn't tell anyone else about the abortion.

"I'm against abortion, but I support a woman's right to have one," I said to my girlfriend.

"That's contradictory. I don't get it. I'd drive myself if I could. I don't want you there," she said.

"I'm going, that's that," I answered.

We didn't speak on the drive to the clinic. After we had parked by the downtown Toledo, Ohio, abortion clinic, an escort in an orange safety vest walked us through an angry mob. The protesters held picket signs and yelled loudly as we approached. Their words were like hatchets that struck deep into my soul. Among the protesters, I saw eyes of anger, eyes of pity, and eyes of shame. A woman protestor who stood near the door in silence caught my attention. The others screamed, but she was calm and didn't say anything. The others seemed out of focus and in a fast motion blur as we were whisked through. The quiet protester was in sharp focus and time seemed to slow down as we approached her, she looked at me with tearful eyes, appearing to have a glow about her. She was a pretty girl, maybe 18 to 21 years old, and she wore glasses. She seemed oddly familiar and then finally she spoke.

"Please," she said, "you would have a beautiful baby, please don't get rid of it." I agreed with her in silence but kept walking. I turned around briefly to look back at her; she stared at me lovingly. I stopped in my tracks. She mouthed something, but I couldn't quite hear it because of the noise from the protesters around us. Did she call me daddy? She walked away and disappeared into the crowd. Trying hard not to be completely freaked out, I kept going. I had helped create life, and now it was being sacrificed for convenience. It seemed to me that it was a time for martyrs and assassins. I looked back one more time to see if I could see the young woman over my shoulder as my girlfriend and I entered the sterile and lifeless looking building. She was gone. I felt so ashamed of myself.

The clinic had prison-like security. From the outside, it looked like a condemned building. On the inside, after passing through some security gates, the lighting was soft and the furnishings tasteful. It reminded me of a fancy tearoom. The nurses were not wearing uniforms–they wore jeans and colorful shirts. Their gentle and encouraging words masked the price negotiations that ensued. To me, there was no disguising the ugly mission of this place. When my girlfriend went into the inner part of the clinic, I sat down in silent thought and sunk deep into the couch of death's waiting room.

The guy sitting next to me felt he needed to talk to me. I hate it when people feel obliged to start unnecessary conversations.

"Yup, second time I've been here. My girlfriend wasn't too excited, but I insisted," he said. He was a forty-year-old guy who should have known better, I thought. There was a quiet imbalance within me as I waited. I can't remember how long I waited but at precisely 4:01 p.m. I felt a terrible pain in my abdomen and my chest. I felt my heart was torn away from its moorings. The pain within my body's core grew as I contemplated my role. Was it another panic attack? A heart attack? I wasn't sure, but then as suddenly as it started, it stopped.

After the procedure, as it was called, my girlfriend and I spoke sparingly. She was waiting for some reaction, but I gave her none.

"What time was the actual abortion?" I asked.

"The procedure was at around 4 o'clock, I guess. Why?"

"That's what I thought," I said. My girlfriend looked at me for further explanation, but I didn't offer any. Our blood had been swept away, suctioned into oblivion, nameless, faceless, not known or touched with warmth. Whispers of daddy fell from phantom lips. My new son or daughter, who would now be 26 years old, was gone forever. I had felt his or her pain of death, and I still mourn the loss to this day. Yes, I support a woman's right to choose, but I think we need to be clear about what we're doing and not hide behind slogans and euphemistic language. I'll never put myself in that position again because I've taken responsibility.

COFFEE CUPS AND VIKINGS

In 1992, I traveled to Norway to conduct research for my doctoral dissertation. I visited the Defense Department Archives, the National Archives, and the Labor Party Archives. I chose to write my dissertation on Nordic foreign policy during the Cold War and how the five Nordic countries balanced their security interests in relation to pressure from the two superpowers. I compared this Nordic Balance to a human hand. Each finger (like each Nordic country) has the capability to move independently of the others, adjusting its movement forward and backward, up and down. Each of the five fingers is attached to the palm, which simultaneously allows for this articulation and provides the security of a base.

I was so focused and busy with my research that I didn't thoroughly appreciate being in Norway and exploring my roots. After completing my research, I took a flight to northern Norway where my father lived. Since my mother's death in 1990, dad would stay in Norway for the spring and summer and then return to Seattle for the rest of the year. Norway is a land of mountains and ocean. The land meets the sea through deep fjords that carve far inland. It's also a land of small farms and towns. The pace of life up north is slow. People have time to live and to know one another. When I arrived up north and was away from the urban Oslo environment and the pressure of my research, I had time to consider my heritage. I thought about how my roots stretched across the seas, thousands of miles, and many years ago. Since I was a little boy, I've dreamed of returning to live in Norway. Mom and dad had made a life for us in the new world. I'm of the new world, but because I grew up with Norwegian language, customs, and traditions, I'm part of the old as well.

When I arrived in Andøya Island, 200 miles above the Arctic Circle, my dad said that we should take a walk up to the graveyard at the base of the mountains. We started out by hiking directly from the back of our property and straight up. The island with its mountainous spine is covered by peat bogs and little birch trees. As we worked our way through the birch forest, we saw the road that led to the village cemetery. We spent about 15 minutes at the graveyard visiting the graves of my eldest brother Bjørn, my grandparents, and my mother. Dad had purchased a double headstone, so there was room for his name when the time came. I couldn't think of a more peaceful and beautiful place to be buried—nestled amongst the birch trees, under the mountains, and overlooking the fjord.

"Let's go," Dad said as he hurried out of the graveyard and headed further south on the dirt road. It was all I could do to keep up with this 77-year-old man. We crossed the Åse River named after the village and then came to a clearing with a gently sloped mound in the middle.

"Oh, this is where we have the midsummer bonfire," I said.

"Ya, and it's also where our ancestors are buried," said dad. I looked at him with curiosity.

"We were just at the graveyard," I said.

"Before there were Christians, people were buried here, on Dungen, they were Viking people," dad said with pride.

"Dungen?" I asked.

"Ya, that is what we call this place," he said in Norwegian.

"So, these are my Viking ancestors?" I asked.

"Ya," he answered. I walked to the top of the mound, and suddenly I was overwhelmed. I felt the sea breeze from the fjord and heard the ageless whispers of my ancestors, and I was at home. For the first time, I realized what this special island meant to me. It wasn't just the island where my parents, my eldest brother, and my sister were born; it was my spiritual inheritance and my destiny. I felt a sacred connection as I stood on the burial mound of my forbearers from 1000 years ago. My dad knew, he had planned this, but he wasn't done.

"Let's go," he said as he took off at a quick pace. We continued south until the dirt road hugged closely to the steep mountainside.

"There it is," he said as he pointed to a group of stones on the slope.

"That is the spot where your mom and I made coffee and ate lunch on warm summer days during haying season," he remarked with sadness. By hand, they would cut the grass and dry it on wire fences. After the grass had dried and turned to hay, they would collect it and store it in their barns to feed their animals for the winter. Dad walked up to the pile of stones and knelt.

"We used these to surround the fire," he said.

"Are you sure it's the same spot?" I asked. Dad ignored my question as he dug beneath the stones, a man in his twilight years unearthing his cherished memories. He dug through the grass and a half-century's worth of dark, fertile soil as I stood and watched. From the hole he had just dug, he produced some charred sticks.

"These were from our campfires," he said.

"Wow, that's amazing," I said. Then, from the hole, dad pulled out a piece of broken, off-white porcelain. It was a handle attached to half of a coffee cup. He gathered a few more pieces and laid them out on the stones in the sun.

"This was one of the cups your mother and I used," he said as he was overcome with emotion, a tear running down his cheek.

"I remember, your mom accidentally dropped the cup and broke it," he said with a smile. We stood and stared at the broken coffee cup, its white ceramic stained by the soil. I imagined the cutting of the hay on those steep sunny slopes so long ago. I saw their small fire and the boiling water. I saw my father as a young man, teasing my mother, as he so often did later in life. I could hear my mother's voice, speaking in their unique dialect, as I pictured them in their youth. Then my father put the coffee cup back into the hole and carefully covered it.

"Shouldn't we take it home and keep it?" I asked.

"No, it's best to leave it here. It belongs here," dad remarked solemnly. My father had finished teaching me.

It wasn't unusual that I would use a hand to symbolize my doctoral dissertation. Hands are remarkable, and I believe everyone's hands tell a story. One of the things I remember most about dad were his hands. He had powerful hands. Decades of hard labor in fishing and construction had made them that way. They were hands that rubbed my forehead when I was a little boy with a fever and they were the hands that spanked me when I misbehaved. They were the hands that provided for us as a family. I watched his hands as he re-buried the broken coffee cup, although they were still strong, they had begun to shake sometimes, revealing his advanced age. I learned of rock and soil, flesh and blood, distant memories, and sacred moments that day. We stood for a while looking out over the fjord as the wind blew and time ticked away ever so slowly and steadily.

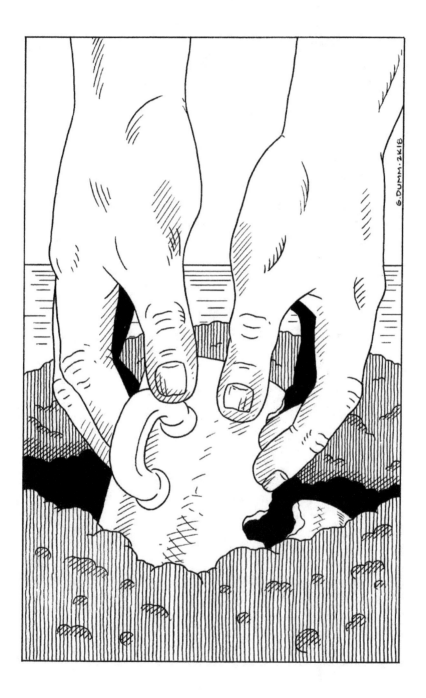

TREETOP WARRIORS

I met Charlotte in graduate school during my separation and divorce from Anna. We quickly moved in together. We decided to move to Seattle in the Fall of 1992. I had already finished my doctoral studies and successfully defended my dissertation, so it was only a matter of waiting to graduate in the Spring of 1993 officially. My two older boys, Bjørn and Byron, stayed behind with their mother in Bowling Green, Ohio. Leaving them behind was one of the hardest things I had ever done in my life, but there were no jobs in Bowling Green, and I had lost custody of my boys in the divorce. Charlotte and I lived with my father in Kenmore, Washington, and then eventually found an apartment in Redmond, right next to the Microsoft campus. I was teaching part-time at Seattle Central Community College, and Charlotte was cleaning houses.

In June 1993, we went camping in the mountains. I decided that Olallie Lake campground near Mt. Adams would be a great place to camp and hike. We set up camp and the next day we hiked up to the snow line on Mt. Adams and sunned ourselves on the rocks. It was a glorious day, we could see Mt. Rainier, Mt. St. Helens, Mt. Baker, and Glacier Peak, in the distance. We decided to go cross-country and not follow the main trail on the way down. We eventually followed a small animal trail, and it was on the edge of that trail that I found an odd object. It looked only like a twisted root at first, but upon further inspection, I saw that it looked ancient and, there was evidence of human shaping of the object. Half covered by debris; I assumed it had been there for ages. The closer I looked at the object the stranger it appeared. It was a human figure, a male figure.

"What do you think it is?" I asked.

"I don't know. Maybe you should leave it here," said Charlotte. I shook my head no and put the object in my pack, and we headed down to the camp. We made a fire, cooked some dinner, and then sat around the fire relaxing. I had the object in my hand and examined it as the evening passed. Finally, it was time for bed.

Later that night I fell into an uneasy sleep. About midnight I woke up because I heard some strange noises like people chanting. I woke Charlotte up and asked her if she had heard anything, but she had not. The chanting sounds grew louder than before, I got a weird tingling sensation coupled with a feeling of hyper-awareness. Maybe the earthly and spirit worlds were colliding, I thought. I put my pants back on, unzipped the tent flap, and sat on my sleeping bag staring out into the starry night holding the strange object that had been in my pants pocket when we went to sleep. I started speaking in a peculiar way that freaked out Charlotte.

"The ancient people, the grandfathers, and grandmothers awaken at night," I said.

"Stop it, you're scaring me," said Charlotte.

"The ghost moon calls," I said as I pointed to the starry sky and the full moon that had an unusual aura. I looked at Charlotte and held her hand to reassure her.

"I'm not sure what's going on," I told her, "I think I hear the voices of ancient Indians."

"You mean Native Americans," she said, correcting me.

"Sure, whatever" I said.

"I see several Indians moving around a campfire," I said.

"I don't see any Indians, ah, Native Americans," she said correcting herself mid-sentence. The trees stood and witnessed as the ancient people began their dance. I could hear a distant drum.

"Do you hear it?" I asked.

"Do I hear what?" she asked.

"A heartbeat and a drum," I said. Charlotte was looking at me like I was crazy, but the vision continued. The fire-shadows grew tall in the trees as the ancient Indians danced around the campfire. I could make out the words that they sang, and I repeated them.

"Ohh Wahh Tay, Ohh Wahh Tay, Kom Sa Yeay, Kom Sa Yeay," I sang as I joined in.

"Look," I said, "they're rising to fill their fire-shadow."

"You're kidding, right?" Charlotte asked. The ancient warriors then flew to the treetops. I could see them move off toward the mountain. A procession of treetop warriors. I explained this to Charlotte, but she said she didn't see or hear anything and was tired.

After a few minutes, I heard another voice, a man's voice speaking in English.

"My name is Leon; I'm a medicine man," he said. I looked all around but didn't see him; I only heard his voice.

"We're having the same vision," he said.

"What's going on?" I asked.

"The ancient ones follow the treetop aerial pathways," he said.

"Where are you?" I asked. Nothing, just silence. I didn't hear any more. Then, off in the distance toward the mountain the Indians call Pahto or Klickitat, and gliding through the night, the starry night, the ghost moon night, the treetop warriors faded away.

When we returned home, I called the Yakama tribe. Their reservation was very near the spot where we were camping. A lady from the Yakama Cultural Center answered, and I told her about the object I had found and my vision.

"We don't know anyone named Leon," she said in a laconic voice.

"He's a medicine man," I said. There was a long pause.

"No," she said.

"Are you sure that..." I was beginning to ask when she interrupted.

"Where's the artifact?" she asked.

"I have it right here in my hand," I answered.

"People often take sacred objects from our land," she said.

"I'm sorry...I didn't mean..." I said.

"Put it back," she insisted.

"You don't want to study it?" I asked. No answer, then she hung up the phone. Charlotte looked at me sympathetically.

"You should put it back, even though I don't really believe in all of that stuff," said Charlotte.

"I don't have the luxury of believing or not believing. These things happen to me whether I want them to or not," I added.

I kept the object but fully intended to go back to Mt. Adams to return it. In the next three years, I had a series of bad luck incidents. Charlotte and I were fighting and arguing, we were having money problems, and we wandered from place to place, not able to settle down, even though we were in a committed relationship. I didn't want her to leave and go back to Norway.

Ultimately, I started a relationship with the woman who would become my next wife, Heather. That was the end of my rocky relationship with Charlotte. I take the blame. Charlotte returned to Norway. Heather and I got married soon after. We also had a baby right away, my daughter Caitlin. By that time, we were living in Auburn, and I was teaching at Green River Community College. Although I was hoping for the best, it wasn't long until my relationship with Heather began to deteriorate, my fault, and I was miserable again.

One day I saw the object I had found on Mt. Adams as we were packing to move yet again. I thought about everything that had happened since I found it. Nothing had gone well. Out of frustration, I threw the object up into the attic space above the attached garage in our rental house. I assume it's still there today unbeknownst to the homeowners or renters.

WILLY

My dream of college teaching came true when I started as a part-time instructor at Seattle Central Community College in the Fall of 1992, but I continued to apply for full-time work. One full-time job that I interviewed for was in Barrow, Alaska. Exactly 15 years after that short summer that I worked in South Naknek, Alaska, I arrived in the North Slope, the ice frontier. When my plane landed in Barrow, I was shocked at the condition of the place. My first impression was that Barrow was the most run-down, messy town that I had ever seen. The houses were little more than glorified shacks with no paint, just worn and weathered boards. And there was junk strewn everywhere, old cars, washers, and other assorted pieces of trash were just a few items. The roads were dirt, and dust blew over everything leaving a fine light brown coating on the entire town. Later I figured out that the severe weather would strip paint off the walls of the buildings, so it was useless to spruce up your house.

Barrow is the northernmost town in North America. The Arctic ice hugged up against the beach year-round. Barrow had grown remarkably since the 1970s with the opening of the north slope oil drilling at Prudhoe Bay. The townspeople were mostly Inupiat (who used to be called Eskimo). One of the teachers at the college met me at the airport. He told me a little about the town and then put me up in the Arctic Hotel. It looked like a hotel from an old western movie. My window overlooked the beach and the ice. The Inupiat People that I had seen since my arrival impressed me with their calmness and smiles.

It was about 11:30 p.m. when I decided to take a walk. It would be light all night, so I didn't have to worry about it getting dark. I walked down by the shoreline and noticed how dark and coarse the sand was. I wandered down the beach for a while, leaning into the gusty, freezing wind. My thoughts drifted back to my walks around the abandoned canneries at South Naknek. Then I heard a voice from the sandy ledge above. An Inupiat man with a black baseball cap smiled down at me as he sat cross-legged on the ledge.

"Where you are standing was the old village," he said.

"Really," I said, "What happened to it?"

"The sea takes away what it gives sometimes," he said with a grin that revealed several missing teeth.

"Come up here and sit for a while," he said.

I climbed the ledge and stood next to the Inupiat man. He was about forty-five years old, short, and had black horn-rimmed glasses. He told me his name was Willy.

"Are there polar bears around here," I asked. Willy looked at me with another big grin.

"There is a big one about one hundred yards away sniffing you now. You were polar bear bait for sure on the beach," Willy said. We shared a laugh, although mine was a bit nervous.

"Here, I'll share this spot, the turf keeps you warm," he said pointing to the grass patch where he sat. I sat down next to him in a cross-legged fashion and felt warmer. I had a strange feeling that he knew that I was coming. After I told him my name, he began to tell me stories about living in Barrow. I knew that these stories had a purpose. They seemed to have no real endings or beginnings. He taught me about the ice flows and whale hunting.

"The Inupiat believe that you had to be good people to get a whale. The whale gives himself to good people," he said. I had been against whaling, but I found his explanation of the sacred hunt satisfying.

"The whale respects good people and rewards them with his body to sustain life," he continued.

I was surprised to learn that Inupiats didn't swim. They would hunt whales in tiny sealskin boats, and if they fell out, they would drown.

"The Great Spirit would take you when he wanted to, it didn't matter whether you could swim or not," said Willy.

Willy seemed to be about my brother's age, so I asked if he was a Vietnam War Veteran like my brother. Willy told me that he didn't like to talk about the war.

"The Army took me from my grandfather and the ice flows and put me in a hot steamy jungle; it was alien to me. I could only hear my grandfather's heart, and when I returned, he was gone," he said while a tear ran down his weathered brown cheek, as he looked out over the ice flows.

He then began to ask me questions about what he had told me. I remembered most everything.

"Which way is north?" Willy asked. I pointed in the wrong direction.

"You are lost," he scolded as he moved my hand so that it was pointed north. "Remember, north is where your heart leads you," he added.

I told Willy that I had to get back to the hotel room. As I stood up to go, he made a circular motion with his hand.

"All the living creatures, the water, and the land are as one," he said. I've met some remarkable people in my life, and

Willy is one of the most remarkable. I believe that my guardian angel had a hand in my meeting Willy. Not only did he possibly save my life, but he also taught me some valuable lessons. Later I learned that American humorist Will Rogers had died in a plane crash in Barrow in 1935. "I never met a man I didn't like" was his famous dictum. Will Rogers had always been one of my favorite Americans. Will and Willy both had something to teach me. I didn't get the job in Barrow, but the experience left me feeling closer to my destination in life, although I still had a long way to go.

FLY ME TO THE MOON

All wasn't well in 1994. Although I had graduated with my Ph.D. in History from Bowling Green State University, a dream that had begun with me writing the letters Ph.D. after my name in my notebook as I sat in a prison guard tower in Mannheim, West Germany in 1979, my personal life was a complete mess. I met Charlotte, a Norwegian exchange student, in graduate school and we had become roommates. I wasn't happy, and truthfully, I missed my boys too much. Consequently, I wasn't a good boyfriend. I was a good roommate though, I always paid my share of the bills. I thought that I loved Charlotte, but it was more out of a sense of dependency. I had the same problem in my previous relationships. I didn't really know what love was. I didn't show my girlfriends and wives the respect they deserved. I had struck up a friendship with a girl named Laura at Seattle Central Community College where I was teaching, and I wanted it to be more than just a friendship. Laura was fun to be with, she made me laugh, and she was of creole heritage. I had begun to fall in love with her, and unfortunately, Charlotte knew that to be true and it was driving her crazy.

One afternoon, I returned from a movie date with Laura. I didn't tell Charlotte where I had been, but then the phone rang, and Charlotte answered. It was Laura. They exchanged some pleasantries, and then Charlotte gave the phone to me along with an angry look.

"I had a good time with you," Laura said.

"Me too," I said.

"Nothing is going to happen because you're already in a relationship, Bruce," she told me.

"I know," I said.

"I don't do affairs," Laura added. Charlotte was in the kitchen listening.

"I could see us being together if circumstances were different," Laura said.

"I know, can I call you later?" I asked.

"Sure, ciao," she answered. I hung up the phone, and then Charlotte was right in my face.

"What did *she* want?" demanded Charlotte.

"Nothing," I answered.

"I'm not an idiot," Charlotte said as she threw down her dish towel. I heard her in our bedroom banging around, then she emerged with her overnight bag, and left in a hurry. I thought about what a jerk I was. Why could I not come clean with Charlotte and tell her that living together was a big mistake? We should have just remained friends. We were good friends. I was a coward who couldn't be honest with her or with myself.

Charlotte and I were living in an apartment in the East Lake neighborhood of Seattle, two blocks up from the Lake Union houseboats made famous in the Tom Hanks movie *Sleepless in Seattle*. Later that same evening, I had already gone to bed when Charlotte came home. My cat Malcolm was sleeping next to me. I could hear Charlotte moving around the apartment, but she didn't come in to check on me. I could hear that she was making tea. Then, she began to draw a bath. I could smell candles burning. Maybe she was just trying to relax. After about 5 or 10 minutes I started to hear Charlotte sobbing. I got up under protest from Malcolm and stumbled across the hall to the bathroom. There, in the candlelight, Charlotte was gently sobbing, barely conscious, and lying in the tub filled with bloody water. She had sliced her left wrist and was holding the extra large butcher knife in her right hand. I got the knife away from her and threw it on the bathroom floor. I then checked her wound and stopped the bleeding with a towel. I replaced the bathroom towel with some surgical dressing from the bathroom cabinet. The bleeding stopped. She was lucky, another few minutes and she would have been dead. I helped Charlotte get up, got her a robe, and hugged her. We were both crying. It was then that I noticed a scrawled note on the floor. I called 911, held Charlotte, and read the note. It didn't make much sense, but I knew this was all my fault.

Charlotte eventually ended up in the psychiatric unit on the seventh floor of the University of Washington Hospital in Seattle. I went to visit her several times. She was making progress and even made some friends in the unit. One day I came to visit her, and we sat in the recreation room. As we were talking, I saw a thin man in a robe trying to put a puzzle together. He was ranting and raving. Then he began playing a small keyboard and singing loudly and off-key. His thinning light-colored hair shot off in all directions, and he wore large wire rimmed glasses that were bent and tilted a bit. Other patients and visitors tried to ignore him even though it was hard not to notice him. I avoided eye contact, but he still approached me.

"I'm George. They say I'm crazy, but I'm not. I'm the sanest person in here," he sang as he skipped around the table and laughed.

"Let me and Bruce talk," said Charlotte.

"Yeah, sure, go ahead, talk, see where that get's ya," he said with a big laugh. Another one of the patients, an older lady, looked at us and smiled.

"He's the good boyfriend," she said as she took her magazine and left the room. I felt guilty about her saying that because I wasn't a good boyfriend. George then gave up his keyboard playing and skipped out of the room which gave us a few moments to ourselves.

"They say I can have an outside pass today, but we can't leave the hospital grounds," said Charlotte.

"That's great," I said. Charlotte got up and talked to the nurse who gave her a badge and a permission note. She grabbed her jacket, and we headed to the elevator. We could still hear George ranting and raving down the hallway.

"He's a lunatic," I said.

"He sometimes steals the women's nightgowns and wears them," said Charlotte.

"Really?" I asked.

"Harmless, though," added Charlotte with a smile. It was good to see her smile. We gave the permission slip to the guard at the elevator door, and he unlocked the elevator and pushed the button. I was holding Charlotte's hand; she seemed at peace as we got into the elevator.

"You know, I'm really sorry for acting the way I have, you deserve better," I said. Charlotte just smiled. We got out of the elevator on the main floor of the hospital and started for the exit doors.

"You are who you are; I am who I am. I just have to accept that," Charlotte said. Just then we saw a thin man in a hospital robe and slippers approach us. It was George, the crazy guy from Charlotte's psychiatric wing. He was accompanied by two beautiful women, one on each arm.

"Hi neighbor," he said joyfully. Charlotte and I were stupefied.

"George, did you get a pass?" she asked. I noticed that he didn't have the badge required for leaving the floor.

"No, they won't give me one. The bastards!" George yelled.

"Then how did you get down here so fast from the seventh floor?" Charlotte asked.

"I flew," he said as he flapped his arms like wings and laughed hysterically. He then proceeded toward the elevators on the other side of the first floor of the hospital.

"Toodle-oo," he added over his shoulder as his companions giggled wildly. I looked at Charlotte.

"Isn't there just one way off the Psych Floor?" I asked.

"Yeah, you have to go through the guard by the elevator," said Charlotte.

"So, no emergency stairs or anything?" I asked.

"I suppose so, but they would be locked and controlled by the guard too," she answered.

"Then how in the hell did he get down here?" I asked.

"I don't know, someone must have let him in," she answered. But me, I couldn't let it go.

"And even if he did use the stairs, he couldn't have come down here that fast and be walking from the exit doors toward us," I added.

"I know, it's weird, but maybe he has a twin" she suggested.

"A twin, please, and wearing a hospital robe and slippers too?" I asked.

"I don't know," said Charlotte smiling.

"And how did he get those two women to come with him," I said.

"Maybe they're nurses," suggested Charlotte.

"Those were not nurses; they looked like exotic dancers," I said.

"I know, it's strange," said Charlotte.

"Strange? It's impossible," I said.

"If you are so concerned maybe you should say something to one of the security people," suggested Charlotte.

"Oh no, I'm not going to fall for that, next thing you know I'll be locked up too," I said.

We continued outside into the sunny day and found a bench in the garden where I sat to gather my thoughts. I picked up a newspaper lying on the bench and read that rock star Kurt Cobain from the band Nirvana had attempted suicide in Rome.

"Maybe he did fly," suggested Charlotte. I just stared at her in disbelief. Less than a month later, Kurt Cobain succeeded in killing himself when he blew his head off with a shotgun in his Seattle home. I had a vision with Kurt Cobain after his death.

"Be yourself, don't try to be somebody else," Cobain told me—sage advice from beyond the grave.

HOMELESS VETERAN

It was another gray, rainy, fall day in Seattle in 1994. I was nearing the end of my relationship with Charlotte and had already started a new relationship with Heather. I was just like the United States in this regard: We never heal from one war before we're in another one. I didn't heal from my last relationship before I was headlong into a new one. I dragged all my emotional baggage with me. I had started teaching a *Vietnam War History* course at Green River Community College and met my Vietnam War Veteran friend David Willson. David and I have been friends for 22 years now. He is one of the most well-respected Vietnam War novelists in America. David is also a great poet, and the go-to bibliographer of the war. He is also my writing mentor. My brother Alf also helped me put the war into perspective, so I felt confident when I got the privilege of teaching the course. I also got a temporary teaching gig at Pacific Lutheran University. Professionally I was doing fine, but my personal life was a chaotic, emotional quagmire.

One afternoon, I was strolling with Charlotte, while we were still living together, on the waterfront in Seattle trying to build up the nerve to tell her about Heather when I walked past a hideously scarred homeless man who was sitting on a street corner by the Public Market. He sat next to a cardboard sign that read: "Pete—Vietnam Veteran." His face looked like it had been badly burned. Pete's legs were crossed, and he was looking down, his dirty jeans were tattered, and he was wearing jungle boots that may very well have begun their journey in Vietnam.

He wore a faded blue baseball cap, and his long graying hair fell to his shoulders. Pete's field jacket was covered with dark greasy blotches. Just as I was about to look away again, he tipped his head up and smiled at me. I smiled in return as I put a couple of bucks in his paper cup.

After passing him, I heard a whispery voice.

"Brother, we're all scarred, either emotionally or physically," the voice said. I stopped, turned, and looked back at the homeless man. He couldn't have said it, I thought, his head was down as if he had fallen asleep. Did I imagine the voice? We walked a little bit farther and then I looked back at Pete again and saw that he was looking at me. I felt a burning sensation inside of my body like I usually do when something bizarre or unexplainable happened.

"Did you hear that?" I asked Charlotte.

"What?" she asked.

"That homeless guy said something," I answered.

"He didn't say anything," she said. We continued walking. Later I told Charlotte about Heather, and we had an ugly fight. She was done with me and moved out not long after. We never recovered from that. Homeless Pete had reminded me that not all scars are visible. He would be one of many people I would meet that would teach me about the Vietnam War, the nature of war, and life in general.

HUEY TURNS BACK THE CLOCK

In 1994, I started teaching a *Vietnam War History* course at Green River Community College. The old theatre style classroom had been used by a previous teacher named Nigel who taught the Vietnam class. He was very popular with the students but quite controversial with the administration. One day he rode his Harley motorcycle into the classroom. My dear friend David Willson also taught in the same classroom. He was a Vietnam War Veteran and taught a *Vietnam War and the Media* course.

The circumstances by which David and I met were rather unique. David had been very upset with an instructor who used the classroom before him. That instructor regularly left the overhead projector out in front of the classroom. One day, David had had enough, grabbed the overhead projector, and threw it into the storage closet in anger. The projector was dashed to pieces, much to the amusement of his students, and it never again plagued David. Later, after I got to meet David and we forged a friendship, we discovered that the annoying instructor who was driving David crazy was indeed me. We've laughed about that ever since.

That classroom had witnessed many years of Vietnam War stories, imagery, discussion, and heartache. After my relationship with Charlotte was beginning to fail, the course that I taught on the Vietnam War took over my life. I had nightmares, emotions evoked in the class carried over into my dreams and came out in strange ways. The theme of tragedy runs through all those dreams. Each day in class a mini drama played itself out. The veteran who tortured himself by taking the class, tears flowing in silent agony, or the son or daughter of a veteran watching a film of their dad torching a village, those scenes occurred regularly. The image and sound of the Huey Helicopter were always in the background. Even the classroom where I taught the class had ghosts.

In teaching the Vietnam War course, I felt an awesome responsibility. My brother Alf was a Vietnam Veteran, and so was my friend, David. In preparing to teach the course, I began to examine my life in the 1960s and 1970s and how the war affected me—I had never really realized how much it had. I was nervous and excited about my first day teaching the course.

I thought I would start the class off with some video comedy. Comedy is a powerful teaching tool because just beneath the surface of comedy is tragedy. I chose clips from Eddie Murphy's movie *Trading Places* and Rodney Dangerfield's *Back to School*. I noticed that one man who sat in the back of the class wasn't laughing at the humorous scenes, as were the other students. In fact, he looked very agitated. I finished my first-day routine, discussed my teaching philosophy, and as I released the class he came up to see me. Some students lingered as he approached and began to speak.

"That film clip showed something that I just can't tolerate," he said.

"What was that," I asked hesitantly.

"I can't stand imposters . . . people who say that they were soldiers when they were not. That makes me God damned mad!" I could see that he was in his late 40s and that he was in a great deal of pain, perhaps both mental and physical. He implied that I was lying when I had said that I was a veteran. I told him that I had indeed been in the Army and wouldn't lie about that. As luck would have it, I had my DD Form 214 (Army discharge certificate) with me that day. It was a coincidence because I was making a copy of it to send in with a job application.

"I've put lots of imposters in the hospital," he said, "and I'm not afraid of the law." He was getting angrier and began inching closer to my face. His eyes were bulging, and his fists began to squeeze harder. Without any further hesitation, I produced the document and gave it to him. He examined it closely and carefully. My adrenaline was pumping as I thought about how I would protect myself and the remaining students in the classroom. Then his shoulders heaved downward as if his anger had been released through a relief valve. He looked at me with sorrowful eyes and said:

"My twin brother died in Vietnam; this is serious shit to me." He never came back to the classroom.

The professor who taught the course before I did was so obsessed by the class that he lived in the 1960s all the time. With a headband around his gray hair, his outrageous do your own thing attitude, and his pot smoking, he was trapped in the 1960s. He died in 1989. No one taught the course after that until I resurrected it for our department. The room had a historic feel. There was a familiar sound in the room that I noticed the first day I was there–it sounded like a Huey Helicopter. I had flown Hueys in flight school. After a few weeks, I tracked the sound to its source. The sound came from the back of the room by the clock. The clock hands didn't move with a ticking sound, rather, they moved with the distinctive 'whop, whop, whop' sound like the rotors of a Huey.

My brother came into the class often to show slides and talk. His oral history presentations helped him heal and provided me with great insights into the war and how it affected him, me, my family, and our country. I was able to understand better how I came to join the military and how the war had shaped my life. Watching him present his story and show his slides brought me back to those times when I felt proud of him serving his country and afraid that he wouldn't return home. When Alf spoke to my class, I saw that the fears were still there. The presence of my mom was overwhelming in those memories as they unfolded in the form of slides and his matter of fact narration. And then there was the clock, with its constant, 'whop, whop, whop.' The Huey rotors were still turning, still reminding us, and still drawing us back to that faraway place in all of us—Vietnam.

BILL BLACK HAWK

I first met Bill Black Hawk in 1996. It was an eventful year: My daughter Caitlin was born, my father's health was declining rapidly because he was plagued by both Alzheimer's and Parkinson's, I left Charlotte, and I married Heather. My good friend David Willson introduced me to Bill Black Hawk who is a Lakota Sioux. Bill wrote a unique book about the Vietnam War called *Red and Yellow*. It was one of the few books on the war written by a Native American. David used to arrange a Viet Nam War Writers' Symposium every year, and Bill was one of the readers. I was very impressed with his story and story-telling. David and I were invited to Bill Black Hawk's birthday party, and all the guests had to bring a poem or short prose piece to read, no presents. I thought it was a good idea. I got into poetry very seriously in 1995, although I had written poems since I was a teenager. There were neo-beat poetry open mic readings in Auburn and Tacoma. It was a fun, creative, and inspirational scene.

At Bill Black Hawk's birthday party, I asked him if he would do a reading from *Red and Yellow* for my Vietnam War History Class at Green River Community College. Also, I had a more personal reason for having Bill Black Hawk come to my class; I thought it would be an opportune time to discuss these powerfully vivid recurring visions I had been having involving my dad. Because Bill didn't have a car, or couldn't drive, I'm not sure which, I had to pick him up in Tacoma which was a 30-minute drive one way. We sat in uncomfortable silence for most of the trip to Auburn until finally, I broke the ice.

"So, Bill, my girlfriend has been scolding me for saying Indian. She says it's derogatory and I should say Native American. What do you prefer to be called, Indian or Native

American?" I asked. Bill sat in silence for a few moments staring straight forward.

"I prefer to be called Bill," he said laconically. So much for small talk.

We arrived at the college, and I parked on the west side of campus close to my classroom. Bill Black Hawk followed me to the classroom, in silence, and when we entered the theatre style room, Bill took a seat in the front. I did my usual introductory remarks, and then I introduced Bill. Applause. Silence. More silence. He just sat there in the front with his back to the students. After what was probably only 2 minutes but seemed like an hour, he spoke.

"What do you want me to do?" he asked. I was dumbfounded.

"The students have read your book so if you could talk about your experiences in Vietnam and the writing of your book that would be fantastic," I answered. He sat for another minute, not moving, facing forward in silence. We could hear coughing, awkward shuffling of papers, and whispering in the room.

"Whenever you're ready Bill," I said politely just wanting to get this thing over with at this point. He started speaking and told some interesting stories, but the whole time he faced the front and didn't look at the students. Only when the students asked questions did he turn his head, ever so slightly. Finally, thank God, it was time for class to end. There was scattered applause, a few handshakes, and then we were off.

I was determined to get a dialogue going on the 30-minute drive back to Tacoma.

"I was pretty lucky today, I found out that a publisher has accepted my book proposal, my second book," I said proudly.

"Define good luck," Bill demanded. I looked at him rather oddly, thinking he was being tricky or just plain difficult.

"When you get something unexpectedly, or something good happens to you," I said. Bill Black Hawk looked away for a moment; then he raised his hand to scratch his forehead. In his usual, carefully chosen and deliberate speech he continued.

"In a Western sense, yes, but my people think of good luck as being able to help someone." I thought for a long moment, then I understood.

"I've been having these dreams, well, visions really, because I'm awake," I explained.

"Visions, yes," he acknowledged.

"My dad has Alzheimer's and Parkinson's, his health is deteriorating quickly," I said before he interrupted me.

"Yes, yes," he said.

"Well, I see these giant archways, like in the Southwest, yellowish-red sandstone, very powerful" I continued.

"Yes, I see them," he said.

"I'm helping him pass through the arches," I finished.

"Do you succeed in passing through?" he asked.

"I think so, yeah, but he is reluctant," I answered.

"You have been chosen to lead your father into the next world," he said.

"Yeah, I guess I'm the closest to my father, of the three siblings I mean," I said. Then he sat again in silence. Maybe he was sleeping; I wasn't sure because it was now dark. Later, he startled me by speaking loudly.

"When do I get paid?" he asked.

"What?" I asked.

"Paid, for tonight, for the lecture," he elaborated.

"I never said I was paying you, Bill. I've no money to pay you. I figured I had all of the students buy your book and read it, and that would be okay," I explained. He seemed annoyed with my answer and sat in silence until we turned onto his street. I stopped the car, and he got out and then turned around.

"There is a message, a connection to another world in those visions," he said.

"You're a seeker and a person who is gifted with the ability to see visions. You have a purpose and a big responsibility," he added.

"Thank you. Maybe we could talk more about spiritual things sometime?" I asked. Bill Black Hawk looked at me, deadpan expression.

"No," he said as he closed the door with a loud slam. That was the last time I talked to Bill Black Hawk.

I did not handle the grief of my mom's passing in 1990 or my dad's death in 1999 very well. I was emotionally numb. The 1990s were tough. My relationship with Heather began to deteriorate after my dad's passing, eventually leading to a divorce in 2008. I had met my current wife, Ginger, in 2007. I was lucky to meet her. Ginger's patience with me as I worked through my healing process has been nothing short of remarkable. In many ways, she saved me. We were married in 2012. In the Summer of 2016, Ginger and I drove to Arches National Park in Moab, Utah. Seeing those arches had been a dream of mine for nearly 20 years; I wanted to see what would happen if I saw the arches and actually passed through them. I had not had the recurring dreams of yellowish-red sandstone arches since 1999, the year my father died. Those dreams were in color and very detailed. I wasn't disappointed; the arches were beautiful. I passed through several of them, sometimes climbing some treacherous rock falls to get to them. There was no immediate spiritual connection. I wondered why? Had I waited too long? Were there different arches I was supposed to visit? No, this was the place. I've had time to reflect on this, and now I think I know.

I needed to close that chapter of my life. My father had already passed on. This trip was about me. I didn't have to feel bad any longer about making the decision not to attach a feeding tube to my father. I did the best I could, made the best decision I could make. My brother and sister didn't want to make the decision, so it was left to me. Or maybe I needed to go to those arches, so I would be motivated to write this book? It was a staggering realization of multiple dimensions. I needed to pass through those arches perhaps for many reasons; Ginger helped me fulfill my destiny by accompanying and supporting me. Now, I've assumed my father's role. I became a *bestefar* (grandfather in Norwegian) today, November 23, 2016, when my grandson Liam was born. You see, I'm always in the process of becoming.

METEORITE

It was Winter in 1996, and I was driving to work in the early morning darkness. I had gone back to work for Boeing again in 1996 after having left in 1989 to pursue my doctorate. I was a buyer working on AOGs (Airplane on the Ground) emergencies. Our job was to expedite parts to the airlines, so they could get their airplanes off the ground and flying again. It was a high-pressure job. My brother-in-law Carl worked in the same building, and my old boss Hal worked in the same group as me. Hal had been demoted from his management position because of complaints from his co-workers. I knew he was a hard-ass, but I got along with him, probably because he was a Vietnam War Veteran. I didn't like the job, but the people I worked with were friendly.

The office complex was on the Duwamish River in Tukwila, very near the Interstate 5 freeway. I also taught history at Green River Community College at night to help make ends meet. As I headed north on the freeway and was ready to exit, I saw a bright flash and streak of light across the dark sky. It started white hot and then became a cool green color. It was too fast to be an airplane. Was it a UFO? I turned on the news radio channel, and reports were coming in. It was a meteorite, and the news report said that it hit the Earth somewhere near the Canadian border. I thought about that meteorite all day. I had seen shooting stars or meteors before, but never one that had hit the ground. What if a meteorite landed on my car? On my house? One of my loved ones? On me? I couldn't worry about such things; I had enough worries.

"You worry too much," said Mel, one of my co-workers.

"Is it meteor or meteorite?" asked Karen, another of my colleagues.

"A meteor burns up in the atmosphere, a meteorite hits the Earth," I said.

"What about one that's still in space?" asked Rick our boss as he strolled by our large cubicle. We all just looked at him.

"A meteoroid," he said with a smile as he headed back to his office.

"That's why he's the boss," said Mel as we all laughed.

At lunchtime, I was still thinking about the meteorite, so I took a walk along the Duwamish River. I felt a special connection to that meteorite. It had been free to travel the universe and then got trapped by Earth's gravitational field and hit the planet's surface in a brilliant final flash. All of us have free will and are free to roam until inevitably we're all brought down to Earth—the great common denominator of death that awaits us all. How fleeting that moment when it fell from the heavens, as our lives are fleeting. We weren't strangers; we were both travelers and one day my journey will also come to an end. Hopefully, I'll shine with such brilliance prior to my inevitable descent. The rest of the afternoon was rather weird as I couldn't stop thinking about the meteorite.

"Are you okay?" asked Karen.

"Yeah, just thinking," I said.

"About your meteorite?" asked Mel.

"Yeah, it kind of gave me a glimpse of what's to come," I said. My co-workers looked at me and smiled.

After work, I strolled to my car while I was thinking. I had just pulled out of the parking lot and onto Interurban Avenue South when I noticed something unusual out of the corner of my eye.

I felt a strange burning feeling, tingly, and the hairs stood up on the back of my neck. I looked to my left as a car was pulling up next to me at the intersection. The driver looked at me, and his face was on fire. I could see him smiling and staring at me with his fire face and glowing eyes. I'm not kidding, flames and all. I blinked, and then, his face was normal again. It was quite frightening. His car raced ahead of mine as the light turned green. A motorist behind me honked to remind me to get going. Had my deep thinking about the meteorite opened me up to things that most people don't see in their normal waking lives? Maybe a different or new reality? Had the meteorite further awakened and sharpened my perceptions of the paranormal? I don't know. Perhaps.

ME AND MRS. COLBY

I went on a job interview to Colby-Sawyer College in the Spring of 1999. The college is in New London, New Hampshire. I flew directly from Los Angeles to Boston and then took a bus from Boston to New London. When I was dropped off on the highway near the town, I was met by a fellow professor who would serve as my host while I was visiting. As we drove into the city of New London, I noticed how old it was, a typical New England town, like in a Stephen King novel. It was rather spooky because the trees were bereft of leaves as it was April and early enough in the spring for some lingering patches of snow here and there. Expecting to be taken to a hotel in town, I was surprised when we instead pulled up to an old building, possibly from the early 1800s. It stood alone on a large plot of land surrounded by a few very twisted old leafless trees.

"What's this building?" I asked.

"Oh, this is the Old Academy Building. We use it for our out of town guests," he said.

"It's old and beautiful," I said. At that point, I figured that others would also be staying there as well. A shiver ran down my spine as we pulled up and parked in the back of the building. I grabbed my bags as my host stuck a skeleton key in a rusty lock on the heavy wooden door, and then we walked up the creaky wooden staircase to the second floor. The long-standing building had a musty smell but was in excellent condition. My room was the corner bedroom. It was filled with antiques and had, what I would call, a tall grandma bed. My host told me that he would come by to pick me up in the morning or I could meet him at the administration office on campus if I wanted to walk (it was a short quarter mile walk). I told him that I didn't need a ride and would enjoy walking. Finally, I had to ask.

"Where are the other guests?"

"Oh, you're the only one," he said rather matter-of-factly, then left quickly. After he had pulled away, I began to feel very alone. The wind was blowing outside and making eerie whistling noises. It was starting to get dark. I began to unpack my suitcase and was thinking about my teaching demonstration that would be part of my interview the next day. Then, after a few minutes, I went into the bathroom to brush my teeth and wash my face. I felt uneasy as I stood over the sink as if someone was watching me. The faucet and all fixtures were antique and in superb condition. Then I decided to look around a bit. The upstairs had accommodations for six guests. All the guest rooms were equally splendid in terms of antiques and general condition. The large upstairs meeting room had a gallery of old portraits on the walls and many long wooden tables and chairs. Most of the portraits were of dour old New Englanders that I chose not to examine closely. I went back to my room and started to read *The Tin Drum* by Günter Grass. Then I heard what seemed like creaking noises from the wooden floors. I dismissed this as just settling noises common in many old wooden buildings. Then I heard distinct footsteps downstairs on the wood floor and a faint human voice. I figured my host had come back to check on me. I stood up and walked to the top of the staircase and called out.

"Hello. Is anybody there? No response. I called out again.

G.DUMM.2K18

"Hello, is somebody there?" No response. I then went back to my room and started reading again thinking that my imagination was getting the best of me. Then I heard more voices and chairs moving and sliding about on the wood floor downstairs. I got up and went to investigate, but I saw no one, and the sounds had stopped. I was feeling thoroughly spooked at this point. I called my wife, Heather, on my flip phone and told her what was going on.

"Get out! Right now, get out!" she pleaded.

"I can't, it's dark, and the guy who is my host has gone home. I'm here all by myself. I have nowhere to go. Besides," I told her, "I don't want to seem like a wimp." She thought I was crazy.

I hung up and went back to my room and sat on my bed very uneasily. I tried to take my mind off these peculiar sounds by reading some more, but, there was no let up. The voices started again, this time there were many more, all coming from downstairs. It was as if a party was going on. Chairs were sliding, there were footsteps on the wooden floorboards, and the voices continued. I got under the covers and pulled them up tight to my chin, hunkered down for what would undoubtedly be a long night. It was at that point that I heard an old Victrola playing music downstairs. There were more voices, more chairs moving, and more creaky footsteps. I sprang up from my bed.

"Stop. Stop it now!" I cried out. I went halfway down the staircase to investigate. By that time the noises and music had stopped. I called my wife again and wanted to document that I wasn't crazy or dreaming.

"Get out!" she kept repeating. Then I climbed back upstairs and went to bed. I slept very lightly and with one eye open all night as the noises randomly continued on and off.

The next morning, I woke up and ventured out of the old building to find some breakfast, but nothing was open. I wandered the streets and looked at all the quaint shops until I finally saw another living soul—a street sweeper. He wore dark woolen clothing and had a very traditional straw broom. He greeted me in his New England accent.

"Morning friend, what are you doing in town?" he asked.

"I'm here for a job interview at the college," I said. The street sweeper looked at me, smiling.

"Is that so? Where are you staying, if you don't mind me asking?" he asked. I turned around and pointed at the Old Academy Building.

"Up there, in the Old Academy Building," I said.

"You're lucky; not many folks get to stay there. Did they tell you it's haunted?" he asked casually. I laughed nervously.

"No, no one told me, and I did have some odd experiences last night," I said.

"It's one of the most haunted places in New England," he said with pride.

"Is that a fact?" I asked.

"Yup. Last week they brought a lady in for an interview and put her up in the Old Academy Building. Well, I'll tell you, in the middle of the night she could take no more of it and ran out into the street screaming for help. They were able to put her in a hotel in town," he said with a smile.

"I can understand for sure. Well, I made it, but just barely," I remarked.

"Good luck to you friend," he said shaking my hand.

"Thank you, have a good day," I said as he walked away to continue with his street sweeping duties. I finally was able to find a coffee shop and got some coffee and a sweet roll for breakfast. I read the local paper and waited. At long last, it came time for me to walk up the hill to the college administration office and meet my host. He greeted me.

"How did you sleep last night? Was everything okay?" he asked. I looked at him carefully for a clue as to his intentions.

"Splendid," I lied, not elaborating on what had happened. I figured that perhaps the haunted building was part of the interview process. We proceeded to go to various meetings with deans and other administrators and some fellow teachers. They didn't ask, and I didn't tell them what had happened the previous night. After that, a formal hiring board interrogated me for nearly an hour. It was then time for lunch. I had a pleasant lunch with the student body president and some of the student government officers. We met in the cafeteria.

"Where you staying?" the bubbly young girl who was the student body president asked.

"The Old Academy Building," I said.

"Wow, I want to stay there," she said.

"Me too," said another girl.

"Yeah, we all want to stay there, but no one's allowed," said yet another girl.

"This whole college's haunted, but the academy building is the most haunted place," said the student body president.

"So, I'm told," I said.

"At least you made it through the night, not like the last person they tried to interview," one of the other students said.

"Well, I really want this job, and I figured it was just part of the interview process," I said with a smile. The students all laughed.

"Hey, I heard Leonard Nimoy and the film crew from *In Search of* came here in the late 1970s to film a special episode," added one of the girls.

"Was it *that* show? I thought it was that other one," said another student.

After lunch, it was time for my teaching demonstration. There were some technical difficulties, and it was delayed for nearly two hours. My host suggested that I take advantage of the downtime to go to the library and look around. I decided to do some research.

Colby-Sawyer College was founded in 1837 when a legislative charter was granted to eleven New London citizens for the purpose of establishing a school in the town. In May of 1838, the academy welcomed its first students. Susan Colby served as the first teacher and principal. She later married James B. Colgate of New York but remained actively involved with the school's progress. This special relationship with the Colby family was formally recognized in 1878 when the New London Academy was renamed Colby Academy. Many people have reported strange paranormal events in the building. Most of these reports came from professors who used the building as temporary housing when they were snowed in at the college, overnight.

After nearly two hours my host came to the library to retrieve me. It was time for my teaching demonstration. It all went well and then it was time to meet the college president. I thought that maybe now they would acknowledge the fact that they had put me up in a haunted building to test me and then offer me the job because of my steely nerves and perseverance. No such luck. There was no mention of the haunted building and no immediate job offer.

After the meeting with the college president, my host met me outside of the president's office.

"How did it go today?" asked my host.

"Oh fine, went well, I'm tired and ready to go home, though," I said. My host winced a little.

"Well, I'm sorry to tell you, but you missed the last bus back to Boston. You'll have to go tomorrow morning. I can put you up in the Old Academy Building again tonight," he said.

I was devastated. Oh great, another night in that spooky old building. What choice did I have? Could I confess my fear and perhaps blow my chances for a job? Or should I tough it out and risk dying from fright? We walked to my host's car and I got in and we drove back down the hill. Another chill ran down my spine as we drove to the haunted building and parked around back.

"I'll see you bright and early, sleep well," he said, probably knowing full well that I wouldn't.

"Ok, thanks. Good night," I said, unenthusiastically. As he drove away I began to hear every creak in that building. Would the second night be worse than the first? I knew only one thing for sure—I was not alone.

It was growing dark and gloomy. There was no moon, and it was overcast. The wind was picking up and I could hear an eerie whistling sound through the eaves of the old haunted building. Dead leaves were rustling on the ground and swirling around the gnarly old trees. I would have to survive one more night and would get a ride at 7 o'clock the next morning.

I hunkered down for the evening once again being the only guest in the Old Academy building. I was ready for sleep, and hoped it would be restful this time.

Not long after I laid down, the sounds began again. First voices, then chairs sliding, then footsteps on the wooden floor downstairs. And then, if that wasn't bad enough, that damn Victrola started playing again. It got louder and louder and louder. I pulled the covers over my head. Then I heard footsteps starting up the creaky wooden stairs; I could hear them coming closer to me. Oh God, will I make it tonight, I thought? I resigned myself to the possibility that the cacophony of noises was probably leading to a crescendo event that I could only in my worst nightmares imagine. Then, suddenly, all was quiet and still. I peeked out from under my covers and saw the room before me; a faint light was coming from a single bulb in the stairway that caused the creepy antique furniture in my room to cast eerie shadows. I breathed a heavy sigh of relief. A few minutes passed where I began to settle a bit.

Then, she came. A ghostly visage suddenly appeared in the corner of my room by the windows. An old woman, in a black dress and bonnet. I was so frightened that I could feel my heart beating in my eyes. She was grim-faced and had her arms folded across her chest. She wasn't happy. She just hovered there, not entirely transparent, but nearly so. She said nothing. My heart was beating so fast I could barely breathe, and I couldn't move. After what was probably only a few minutes, but seemed like hours, she went away. It was quiet and uneventful for the rest of the night. I finally fell asleep, emotionally drained and physically exhausted.

I woke up the next morning and was thankful to be alive. As I packed my things I decided to have one last look around. I looked at the gallery of portraits again, and suddenly my heart stopped. There she was: Susan Colby, the founder of the college. Its first President and teacher. It was she who appeared in ghostly form in my room the night before. I stared at the portrait as her penetrating eyes paralyzed me temporarily. I then heard my host drive up the driveway, I left the haunted building behind. My trip home was uneventful, and a week later I found out that I didn't get the job.

Since my visit, the original New London Academy Building was donated by the college to the town of New London and, after being refurbished, today serves as the community's town hall. Stories of strange happenings and ghosts are still being reported at the site.

A HERO'S JOURNEY HOME

As the wheels of the Boeing 737 touched down on the rain-soaked runway in Seattle, I was jarred back into the present reality. Thoughts and memories about my dad filled my mind during the short flight from southern California–my new home. It was the Fall of 1999, and I had finished graduate school and found a job in California. I was a busy college teacher and dad was proud of me. So why did I feel so guilty? It was true that I didn't live near my father, and I didn't visit him as often as I should. I knew that he spent his days staring out the window of his retirement home room, disconnected from the present, unsure of the future, and desperately clinging to his past. His once powerful hands shook uncontrollably, and his once muscular body was now withered and weakened with age and disease. I feared to see him. I picked up my rental car at the airport and drove to Ballard to visit my father. He recognized me with a smile. We sat down at the kitchen table where the retirement home manager had set out some coffee and sandwiches. We sat in silence for a few moments, then, as he struggled with his shaking hand to bring the coffee cup to his mouth, I saw that his eyes reflected unfamiliarity. I could see him fade out and slip into a combination of vague memories, hazy recollections of past experiences, and uncomfortable emotions as he began to stare into the trembling coffee cup.

"I once had a son who was a teacher and a writer," he said.

"I am not sure where he is . . . he doesn't visit anymore," he continued wistfully, tears forming in his eyes, "do you know him?"

A few days later, Dad was kicked out of his residential retirement home because he kept escaping and because he became hysterical one day. He was convinced that people were going to kill him and all the others in the home. Dad began throwing dishes and yelling in Norwegian. The caretaker called the police and dad was sent in for psychiatric evaluation at Swedish Hospital in Seattle. I talked to the attending doctor.

"What happened?" I asked.

"He got upset and agitated and started yelling and throwing things. No one could understand him," the doctor said. I turned to my father.

"What happened, dad?" I asked. Dad answered in Norwegian then I looked at the doctor.

"Dad thought that Nazis had come into the house and he was trying to protect the people in the home," I said.

"That's very interesting. It's strange how dementia works," said the doctor.

"Well, he did live under Nazi occupation," I remarked. The doctor was taken aback.

"That makes sense. The war is still haunting him, and now it was manifesting itself in his dementia," he said. After dad was released from Swedish Hospital, I found an Alzheimer's facility for him near Lake City Way in Seattle. He only lasted a few weeks there and went downhill very quickly. While dad was degrading rapidly, my brother and sister relied on me to be the emotional head of the family. They told me that I would have to make any decisions about dad and they would support me. I got a call from dad's doctor after I returned to California.

"Your father is dying, he can't eat or drink enough," he said.

"What do we do?" I asked.

"We can insert a feeding tube if you want us to," he answered. I thought for a few moments.

"Is he ever going to get better?" I asked. The doctor paused a long while.

"I don't believe so," he answered.

"My dad was a very proud and active man," I said.

"I understand," said the doctor.

"What would you do, if he were your dad?" I asked the doctor. He took a long time to answer.

"I wouldn't do it," he said.

"Then we won't do it," I said with a lump in my throat. Dad was sent to hospice care in Kirkland the next day.

I was the one who had to make the life and death decision for dad. I had also been the one tasked with taking dad's keys away from him when we determined it was unsafe for him to drive. I was also the one who had to drop dad off at the assisted living home. I still remember what dad told me when I left him at the home. I helped him get situated in his room with some of his things and then it was time for me to leave. He got his hat and coat and was ready to leave with me.

"Dad, you're staying here, you're not going with me," I said. He looked at me sternly and spoke in Norwegian.

"Oh, so you think you're the one in charge now," he said. That wasn't easy. Now, I couldn't believe that I, the youngest child, was making life and death decisions for my father. What authority did I have? Dad was the man who cared for me, the man who rubbed my forehead when I was afraid at night, the man who may have saved my life when I almost ran off of a cliff at Deception Pass on Whidbey Island. He was a larger than life heroic figure for me. Now it was I who had to decide if my father would live or die.

"Are you afraid of dying, dad?" I asked.

"No," said dad, in Norwegian. It was comforting to hear that. That was the last thing he said. Soon after, he slipped into a coma.

I saw my brother cry for only the second time in my life when dad passed away on August 20, 1999, at precisely 8:20 pm (8:20 on 8/20). Dad passed peacefully and naturally, but it was all too much for my sister. The hospice nurse, a middle-aged black man, was an angel during the final hours. He explained the natural death process to me and allowed dad to have the dignity he deserved by removing his oxygen tube when death was imminent. I was holding dad's hand and rubbing his forehead, just like he did for me when I was little. Then he went. It had come full circle. He was my first and greatest hero, and it was time for his final journey.

In September 1999, I flew to Norway with my sister, my brother, and brother- in-law to bury my father. Scandinavian Airlines (SAS) transported dad's casket from Seattle to Oslo, Norway. Then, my brother and I boarded a flight with dad in the cargo hold from Oslo to Narvik. My sister and her husband flew directly to the island where dad was to be buried. Because of the size of the American style casket, Narvik was the farthest we could go by airplane. Just before we landed in Narvik, the flight attendant approached my brother and me.

"You two look alike, are you brothers?" she asked.

"Yes," I answered.

"I heard you two speaking English. Are you on vacation in Norway?" she asked.

"We're here with our father, taking him back home," my brother said.

"Where is your father?" she asked.

"In the cargo hold," I said, pointing down. The flight attendant gasped as she held her hand over her mouth. Then, she excused herself and moved forward to the cockpit area. After a few moments, she came back.

"The captain would like you two to wait on the plane after the other passengers leave." I looked at my brother, and we both nodded yes.

About 30 minutes later we landed, and boy what a landing. The airport at Narvik is nestled between tall mountains surrounding a fjord. The winds were wicked that day, and the plane crabbed into the runway at almost 45 degrees to the port side. Just a second or so before the wheels touched down the pilot turned the nose straight ahead for landing. We bounced around pretty good, and some bags came out of the overhead, and many people screamed in fright. Any landing you walk away from is a good one I was once told by my instructor pilot in flight school. After all the passengers disembarked the captain came back putting on his flight jacket as he walked. He shook our hands.

"I'm Captain Karlson, so your father was from Northern Norway," he said.

"Mom and dad were both from Andøya. We buried mom in 1990; now father's returning home to be buried," I told the captain in Norwegian.

"You speak, Norwegian?" the captain asked.

"Yes, both of us," my brother said.

"I want you to see how good care we take of your father. Come with me," he said. We followed the captain outside. A few moments later a man driving a luggage cart truck arrived and was met by four large baggage handlers and a forklift. My dad's coffin emerged, packed in a crate on a large pallet. The forklift reached into the baggage hold and secured the crate and then gently placed it on the cart, which buckled under the weight. The men then broke apart the shipping container revealing the beautiful dark wood coffin that my sister had bought. The captain then ordered the men to lift the coffin up, so they could slide the pallet away. The four big men struggled to lift my father's coffin.

"Bloody hell," said one of the workers who was immediately admonished by the captain. Apparently, American caskets are very heavy. The captain ran over and helped them. After a few bumps and twists, the men and the captain eased the coffin back down onto the cart. He said a few words to the workers, and they seemed to apologize to him.

"I'm sorry, we want to show respect for your father and his final return home to Norway," the captain said.

"I think dad would have enjoyed the fuss actually," I said.

"Yeah, he had a great sense of humor," my brother added. The captain smiled. We all stared at my dad's casket for a moment, then the baggage handlers dispersed. My brother and I were left with the coffin, the cart driver and the captain.

"That was a tough landing with the wind," I told the captain. He nodded.

"Yes, but not too bad. Try it in the winter with icy runways; now that's some fun I tell you," he said as he laughed. We thanked the captain, and he shook our hands and walked away. The cart truck driver gave us the manifest to sign, and we did.

We followed the cart out to the loading area in front of the small terminal. It was there that we noticed a black funeral truck and two morticians leaning against it smoking and talking.

One was in his 30s, tall, lanky, with short brown hair and a goatee. The other one was older, in his 70s, white long wispy hair. They both wore black suits; the elder mortician's suit was well worn and dusty. The older one motioned to the cart truck driver, and the younger one opened the back of the hearse. It was taller than an American hearse, and more like a delivery truck. The cart driver parked directly behind the funeral truck and got out.

"Hey, give us a hand here," yelled the cart driver to some baggage handlers who were smoking and on break.

"Not necessary," said the older mortician as he waved them off and pushed them aside. He and his son lifted the hefty coffin into the funeral truck with not much trouble. That old man was sure strong.

"You want to ride with us?" asked the younger mortician. I looked in the hearse and saw just two seats in front and dad's coffin in the rear.

"Where would we be sitting?" I asked. The elder mortician tapped the top of my dad's casket and smiled. I thought about it for a few moments then declined. I felt that such a ride would be a bit too macabre, even for me, although I'm sure dad would have thought it was funny if my brother and I had to sit on his coffin for the trip. It was a three-hour drive through twisting turning roads around tall mountains and deep fjords. The hearse pulled away and began its journey to our dad's final resting place. Our bus left 30 minutes later.

At the old farm home in Åse on the island of Andøya where my father was born, my sister and all the other relatives were waiting, including my Aunt Walborg the Nazi collaborator, and Aunt Solbjørg who had lived in our old farm house during the war with her children, my mom and my eldest brother, and my grandparents. My dear Nazi aunt was already arguing with my sister Bjørg, Aunt Solbjørg, and everyone else. It was miserable having to deal with her and the grief of losing my father. My Nazi aunt had made life difficult for my father. Aunt Walborg's collaboration with the Gestapo and subsequent arrest for war crimes after the war had led to my father and mother deciding to come to America. My dad told me that he was tired of hearing comments about his Nazi sister. At the start of our trip to Norway, I had injured my back and was in terrible pain the whole time. When the time came to bury our dad, we carried the massive American casket to the gravesite. Everything was done the old-fashioned way on the island. I was in absolute agony every step of the way.

As we approached the grave that had been dug, I could tell that it was a little narrow for the size of dad's casket. European caskets are what morticians call toe-pinchers and much narrower than rectangular American caskets.

We started lowering the coffin despite the grave being too narrow. We didn't have a winch; we lowered the coffin by hand with ropes. The ropes burned my hands as we lowered dad's remains. The coffin started to go down but then got caught up on some roots. The rope slackened on my side as the casket stopped, but the other side continued downward. Finally, the roots gave way with a loud snap, and the coffin dropped suddenly spraying dirt and rocks high up into the air and then crashing back down onto the casket and the assembled mourners. The bulk of the dirt and rocks fell on Aunt Walborg from Oslo in her prim and proper funeral attire and carefully coiffured hairdo. The look on her face was priceless.

She was horrified and disgusted at the same time. It was all I could do to keep from laughing out loud, and I wasn't the only one holding in my amusement. I assumed that dad enjoyed the spectacle from his perch in heaven since he was quite the practical joker. The incident had quieted my Nazi aunt. She was well behaved for the rest of the day until they left.

In bringing my father home, I had faced the ordeals of his final journey: experiencing his death firsthand and making the big decision, my back injury, the long arduous trip to Norway, the rough landing in Narvik, my crazy Aunt Walborg, and the stubborn defiance when dad's enormous American coffin wouldn't go easily or smoothly into the grave. All of this made sense; a hero's journey isn't easy, and I was there every step of the way, so I could document the experience. My father has visited me on occasion since his death, most recently appearing in our walk-in closet just before we took a trip to the Arches National Park. I believe he has been trying to reassure me that I made the right decision. He is still with me, my hero.

FLIGHT 77

Early in the morning on September 11, 2001, I woke up from a terrible nightmare. The world was crumbling; the Earth was shaking, mountains were collapsing, it was the end of the world. I woke up in a cold sweat, and after a few panic-stricken minutes, I realized it was a dream. I took a shower and got ready to meet my two Citrus College colleagues, Teresa and Eric, for breakfast. We were in Norfolk, Virginia, and were planning on touring Naval Station, Norfolk, the largest naval base in the world. We were working on a project to provide online college courses to sailors deployed on ships. After breakfast, we met the base education center personnel and started our tour. As we got to the static aircraft display by a back gate, some sirens went off, and then a military vehicle pulled up to the gate and dispatched some guards with rifles.

"Something has happened, this isn't just a drill," I told my colleagues. We then walked back to the education office where we found the office personnel staring at a TV screen.

"Terrorists have hit the World Trade Center and the Pentagon," said one lady. I literally fell back into a nearby chair; my first thought was that this was our generation's Pearl Harbor. I thought of my family, my children, were they going to be okay? What could I do? I felt so helpless. Our group remained on base for a few hours; then we had to leave. The ships were getting ready to be deployed, and base security was at the highest level.

We spent Wednesday and Thursday nights in Virginia Beach near Oceana Naval Air Station, waiting for news on airports opening. I watched many navy fighter jets scrambling on their way to deploying aircraft carriers. There was little other activity. No civilian aviation. It was so eerie without hearing airliners overhead. Ordinarily, Virginia Beach is pretty lively because it's a Spring Break destination for college students. We saw no signs of festivities, the people that were there were rather quiet and kept to themselves.

"Let's just drive west," I said.

"Shouldn't we just wait here?" asked Eric.

"No, maybe Bruce is right, our best chance for a flight is further west," said Teresa. We all agreed, but we needed to clear it with the college president, who happened to be Teresa's dad. She got him on the phone and handed it to me.

"You're in charge Solheim, get my daughter, you, and Eric home safely," he said very plainly.

"Yes, sir!" I answered. We figured our best chance was to head to Nashville. There were rumors that it may be one of the first major airports to open again.

On the drive from Virginia Beach to Nashville, we saw many Americans in shock—every place that we stopped to eat, people sat in near silence. American flags hung at half-mast, and small flags flew from the antennas of passing automobiles. The airport at Nashville was filled with police and security personnel who searched all the bags and each passenger. The airport was pure chaos. Everyone was nervous. Although no one talked too much about it, the feeling in the airport was reserved, cautious, and frightened. Making the situation more intense, there was a middle-eastern looking man buying tickets one line over from us. He was wearing traditional Arab clothes. Everyone was watching him. He glared back at us in silent defiance. Then, he moved away from the line and stood by himself. People at the airport encircled him and stared at him. Every set of eyes was on him, and no one said anything. This poor man was receiving all the anger that day.

"I know it's terrible to say, but I hope he's not on our flight," I said to my colleagues. The flight took us from Nashville to New Orleans where we quickly connected to a flight to San Diego. When we landed in San Diego, the flight attendant made an announcement.

"Well, thank God, we made it." The whole plane erupted in applause. News cameras awaited us inside the terminal. It hit me when I finally got home, and we were safe. Everyone was saying that the world had changed. I believe that the world's problems had come home to America. Gone was our feeling of relative safety. I felt an overpowering desire to grab an M-16 and go back into uniform. After I unpacked my bags at home, I looked at my original return ticket. American Airlines, Flight 77, Dulles to Los Angeles, departure 8:20 am, September 12, 2001. That was the same flight that hit the Pentagon. My blood ran cold. Had the terrorists decided to delay one day, Eric, Theresa, and I wouldn't be here; we would have died in the fiery Pentagon crash. We feel a special kinship with those passengers on Flight 77 who didn't make it home safely. Timing is everything. I've since learned that many people had disturbing dreams just before 9/11; I wasn't the only one.

SASQUATCH

Sasquatch, also known as Bigfoot, Skunk Ape, Yeti, and many other names, is an apelike creature and international phenomenon. Most scientists believe that the creature is a combination of folklore, misidentification, and various hoaxes. I had grown up with stories about Sasquatch. I tended not to believe any of those rather tall tales even though I secretly hoped that the creature existed. There was even a professor at Washington State University, Dr. Grover Krantz, who specialized in Sasquatch research. Ridiculed by other academics who tried to force him out and lose his tenure at the university, Grover persisted in his research. I tried to entertain the idea of Sasquatch's existence, kept an open mind, but it was hard to jump on the Bigfoot belief bandwagon. That was, until, the Summer of 2010.

That summer, Ginger and I were driving back from Seattle. It was getting dark as we drove into the Redwood Forest in Northern California. The drive through the coastal redwoods was spectacular and a little spooky. North of Orick on the 101 highway, the roadway was twisting, turning, narrow, and it was extremely dark with massive redwoods towering above us. As I came around a long left-hand bend in the highway, I got a glimpse of something on the right side of the road. I slowed down, and as we approached, I saw a dark figure leaning toward us. It was large, well over six feet tall, and hairy. Wearing a hat, and standing just a foot or two from the edge of the pavement, it just stood there, not the least bit afraid of our truck. It did move its limbs and head slightly and was covered with dark matted hair.

I was in shock, but immediately thought that this creature must be Sasquatch. I woke up Ginger as I accelerated and didn't look back.

"Ginger, I think I saw Bigfoot," I said.

"What?"

"I think I saw Sasquatch."

"Very funny," she said.

"I'm not kidding; it really was Bigfoot, I think." Ginger looked at me, and I couldn't tell if she was frightened by the thought of having an encounter with Bigfoot or the possibility that I was crazy.

"I'm kind of tired, maybe we should stay in Orick tonight," I suggested.

"Where's that?"

"Just another five miles."

"Are you nuts? Keep driving," she said. So, I kept driving for another hour. I was still in shock. I still am bewildered.

Later, after doing some research, I found out that Humboldt County has had the most reported Bigfoot sightings in the United States and many of them have been near Orick. Bluff Creek, only 20 miles from Orick, is where Roger Patterson and Bob Gimlin filmed their famous Bigfoot video in 1967. I realize that by writing these words, I'm admitting that I think I saw Sasquatch and that publishing this story may put me on the shortlist for retirement at my college. But, as they say on Fox News, "we report, you decide." Was it Sasquatch or someone impersonating the creature? I don't know. If this was just some guy dressed up like Bigfoot, why would he risk life and limb standing so close to the highway at night just to perpetrate a hoax?

BREATHE EASY

I loved having a big sister. She was 15 years older than me, and I thought of her as a hip aunt. Every time she traveled, before she had kids, she would get me a Corgi car. I had quite a collection. My favorite car was the Aston Martin DB-5, James Bond car. She divorced her Norwegian husband and then married a Navy pilot named Carl. She had two kids, and they moved to Chicago for a while. They returned to Seattle to live in 1974 and stayed for good. Over the years we had our ups and downs, and we (along with my brother) worked through the death of our mother in 1990 and our father in 1999. From 2003 to 2005 I didn't speak to my sister, I can't even remember what we argued about, but we were both very stubborn. A Solheim family trait, unfortunately. Oddly enough, it was my Nazi Aunt Walborg who suggested that I should reach out to my sister and not wait too long. Despite her past, Aunt Walborg was almost always nice to me, and I think she sought redemption at the end of her life.

The last time I saw my sister Bjørg was at her 70th birthday party in Norway in the summer of 2014. She wasn't well, in fact, she hadn't been well for many years. She had severe breathing problems related to disease caused by many decades of smoking. She could barely walk from the living room to the kitchen. Despite that, we had a great time together. She refused to be sad or give up. After we returned, we talked on the phone, a very serious talk.

"I didn't plan on coming back," Bjørg said.

"Really," I said.

"Yeah. I've lived longer than mom, and I don't deserve to live longer than her," she said as she began to cry. I started crying too.

"Why do you say that?" I asked.

"She was a good person; I could never be as good as mom," Bjørg said.

"You are a great person, and I love you!" I insisted.

"Thank you," she said.

"I want you to be around for a long time. You're my big sissy," I said. I remember that when we were in Norway together, she spent most of her time on the couch in the living room, reading, drinking wine, and talking to visitors. Bjørg was the most social person I've ever known. One of my last memories of her, in Norway, was her listening to the classical music of Norwegian composer Edvard Grieg on the stereo in the living room of our old family home in Åse.

I talked to my sister on the phone once a week. She was very good at staying in touch and checking in on us. I would often bounce ideas off her, and she would give me advice. Whenever I was upset, my sister would say: "Chin up," just like the spider Charlotte in the book *Charlotte's Web*. Her last message to Ginger and me was to remind us to give her a call, and she ended her message by affectionately calling us knuckleheads.

On December 5, 2014, my nephew called and told me that Bjørg had died suddenly while at lunch with her friends. I knew she was very ill, and I can't say that it was a surprise, but it was devastating nonetheless. We had a memorial for her in Seattle and spread some of her ashes at a beach in West Seattle where she lived. We planned to go to Norway in the summer to spread the rest of her ashes. I had a vision of my sister a few days after she died. I saw her running through the grass in front of our old family home in Norway. She was a little girl and was running free and able to breathe easily.

Summer came, and we traveled to Norway to bring my big sister's ashes home. We had a gathering of relatives, my wife Ginger, her mother Mary, and my sister-in-law, Courtney. My nephew Dain put her ashes on my parent's grave. Then, we had fish soup and homemade cheese and herb bread at a pub in Dverberg. Many of the relatives had wine and beer. Bjørg would have loved it.

As we prepared to leave, I decided to sit in my favorite rocking chair and think. I switched on the stereo and listened to Grieg, picking up where my sister left off. Then, it was time to go. I locked up the house and got into the car, and as we drove away, I looked at the window in the laundry room. There she was, my sister, as a little girl with pigtails, peeking through the window at us. Chin up, she was home.

IT'S ALL TRUE

I had known Gene Thorkildsen since we were little boys. Our Norwegian immigrant parents were good friends (his mom was born in the United States and was of Norwegian descent). We grew up together in Kenmore, Washington. I looked up to Gene, like another big brother. He looked out for me, advised me, and made me laugh through tough times in high school. When the Beatles movie *Yellow Submarine* came out in 1968, it was a terrible year in America; the Vietnam War was raging, protesting everywhere, rioting in the streets, cities burning and the tragic assassinations of Dr. Martin Luther King, Jr, and Robert F. Kennedy. I was worried about my brother Alf fighting in Vietnam. Would he come home? The world looked very dark indeed. But one sunny afternoon mom dropped Gene and me off at a theater, I think in the University District in Seattle, to see *Yellow Submarine*. It was great fun, I forgot about all my worries and troubles for a while. We were happy. Gene had reintroduced me to the Beatles.

My brother was a big fan when the Beatles first invaded America. I remember watching them on Ed Sullivan. I've been a fan ever since. We enjoyed the movie, and I'll never forget it. Gene had a knack for always being there when you needed him most.

Gene and his father spoke at my dad's memorial in 1999 and said some comforting, kind, and funny things about my father. Gene's father Leif passed away in 2009. I wasn't able to go to Seattle for his memorial, but I watched it on live video. Gene and I had contact over the years, and I would see him occasionally. We had similar interests. I loved writing plays, and he loved acting and directing. Most of all, we both loved Norway.

In 2013, he wrote me a shocking email. He had been battling lung cancer since October 2012. I was devastated. How could Gene have lung cancer? He didn't smoke. I found out that it was adenocarcinoma, the most common lung cancer for non-smokers. He got through his initial bout with cancer through radiation and chemotherapy and was in remission. In 2014, I contacted Gene about directing and starring in a staged reading of my play, *The Epiphany*. I was able to get the reading set up at the Nordic Heritage Museum in Seattle. Gene assembled several of his actor friends, and I got a Norwegian veteran named Åge Johnny Nabben Olsen to come from Norway and act in the play. It was a great success and Gene was the main reason why. Gene, his mom Beverly, and his sister DeeAnn even made krumkake (a delicious Norwegian cone-shaped cookie) for the audience. His performance was extraordinary. A few weeks later I got a call from Gene while I was at work in my office. He sounded upset.

"What's the matter, Gene?" I asked.

"My cancer's back; it's in my brain," he said with a great deal of emotion in his voice. I was in shock. How could that be? We were just working together in Seattle, and he seemed so alive and healthy. Apparently, his lung cancer had returned and spread to his brain. I tried to be as supportive as I could. He told me that I was the first person he spoke to about his cancer outside of his family.

I reached out to a friend of mine at work who had survived cancer and got some books to read and recommended them to Gene. I think Gene already knew that he wasn't going to make it, but he also wasn't going to let cancer stop him from doing what he wanted to do. As an example of his courage and determination, he competed in the grueling Birkebeiner ski race in Norway. A film crew followed him on that daring adventure. He didn't complete the race, but everyone was impressed with his bravery and tenacity. He returned to Seattle and slowly began to fade, becoming weaker and weaker. Gene passed away on September 14, 2016, the same day I left for Norway to see the full production of my Norwegian World War II play, *The Epiphany*. That Norwegian production wouldn't have been possible without Gene's hard work and belief in the story and his spearheading the staged reading in Seattle.

After I had returned from Norway, I started to think more about Gene. I had tried to put his death out of my mind during the trip, so I could do the substantial work that was necessary for the international production of my play. On October 9, 2016, I had my first vision of Gene. I was lying down, reading, and thinking about him and what a loss it was for his family, for his friends, for me, and for everyone. A kind and gentle soul had been taken from us too soon. In a vision, Gene spoke to me. His hair was long, he was young, he was strong, and he was happy.

"There's no past or future in the afterlife," he said with his characteristically big smile.

"Only the present?" I asked.

"Kind of…everything is light, airy, moment to moment, you know," he said.

"I think so," I said.

"Now that you're dead, are you in heaven?" I asked. Gene smiled.

"Yes, but it's weird to talk about being dead when I don't feel like I'm dead," he said.

"I don't understand," I said.

"Hard to explain, even for me, maybe it would help for me to say that I am, not I was like in the past tense, just that I am, I am present," he said.

"I think I get it," I said.

"It's all true. All of it!" Gene said with excitement.

"What's true?" I asked.

"Do everything to your fullest, put everything into your role in life because it echoes in all of eternity," he said. Before I could fully understand what he had just told me, the vision shifted.

In the next vision, Gene and his father Leif were framing a big house, and it was a beautiful sunny day. Neither one of them were wearing shirts. Gene didn't have shoes either.

"Why don't you have shoes?" I asked. He laughed.

"Don't need them anymore," he said with a big smile. Then the vision shifted again, and Gene and I were in a theater. He was running around very rapidly. I got the impression that he was both directing and starring in the play, but it wasn't clear which play he was directing although the stage and scenery were massive.

"Do you want to stay for rehearsal, it's about to begin," he said.

"Sure," I said. Gene kept moving quickly from place to place not slowing down.

"Could you slow down so I can talk to you, maybe ask some questions?" I asked.

"Too much to do, I don't have to sleep now; I have to keep going," he said. Then he looked at me seriously.

"But you should rest," he said. Did he mean that I wasn't sleeping enough? Is that what he meant. In any event, I've been trying to sleep more.

All of this made me think of time and the passage of time. It's often said that we should slow down, smell the roses and that we've all the time in the world. We're also told that time is running out. What to do? As we grow older, time seems to pass more quickly than when we were young. Technology is supposed to save us time, and time is money, yet we appear to have less time to spend.

But what's real time? I think it's time we spend with friends and loved ones. We should make more of an effort to stay in touch with old friends, relatives, and people we love. They may not be here tomorrow. Throughout my life, and especially as I've grown older, I try to find the constellation Orion when I look at the night sky. It has always been very comforting to me. The story is that Orion the Hunter is forever searching for his lost love. It reminds me of the quests and dreams all of us have in life: for love, for fame, for fortune, for truth, and for happiness. Some of these quests and dreams come true, some don't, and others may drive us mad in the end. The stars at night remind me that one day I'll blend in with those twinkling stars and return to the stardust of which I'm made. I think of my parents, my relatives, my friends, and all of those who came before me when I look at the night sky. I picture that each one of them is a star in an infinite universe. In this endless whisper of time, then, I don't feel so alone.

THE EPIPHANY

I was inspired to write my play *The Epiphany* by the stories my parents told me of living under Nazi occupation. I was also inspired by my cousin Eva Solheim's book—*Lokkeduen og Sjøkapteinen (The Decoy and the Sea Captain)*. My mom and dad were married in January 1940 just three months before the Nazis invaded Norway. My father was forced to work for the Germans, and a Nazi colonel moved into the house my parents shared with my grandparents, my Aunt Sølbjorg, and her children. My eldest brother Bjørn died during the war because the Germans had taken all the medicine. My dad's brother, Thorvald, was a war hero convoy commander during the war, and his youngest sister Walborg was a notorious Nazi collaborator who worked for the Gestapo. My parents decided to move to America largely because of my Nazi aunt and the lack of opportunities in postwar Norway. I can't help but think how different my life would be if there had been no war and my aunt had not decided to become a Nazi, my parents probably would not have come to America. Over the years, I've made many trips to Norway starting with my first trip in 1962 on the Ocean Liner, Stavangerfjord. My brother and I, along with my two nephews, own the old family home and farm in northern Norway on the island of Andøya.

In September 2016, my wife Ginger and I traveled to Norway with 15 student actors and two other faculty members to perform *The Epiphany* for the Norwegian people. It was a dream come true. The spirits on the island and in our little village of Åse were active as soon as we arrived. I could feel the energy in the air and all around me.

"It's like the air is filled with electrical energy," I told Ginger. We settled into the old family farm house and prepared for the whirlwind days ahead. I had to go to rehearsal, so Ginger stayed home. While I was gone, she heard footsteps, a man's footsteps, in the back-entryway room to the house that also doubles as a food storage area and a place to leave your shoes, in Norwegian, it's called a *gangen*. Ginger had a feeling that it was somebody, a ghost presence, so she acknowledged their arrival.

"Hello," said Ginger. There was no answer, but the footsteps continued.

"I'm just trying to clean up and I hope it's okay," she added. No response, more footsteps.

"I'm not afraid," she said. The footsteps stopped. Later when I came home, Ginger told me what happened. I looked at the back entryway. There are several doors to go through to enter the back of our old farm house. There is the outer door that leads to a short hallway that connects to the garage and the inner part of the house. Then there is the door to the back entryway. Then there is the last door to the kitchen. On that last door, there is my father's old nameplate. It reads Asbjørn O. Solheim.

"Was this kitchen door open?" I asked Ginger.

"Yeah, I left it open because I like it better," she said.

"My dad liked that door to be closed. He always yelled at me for leaving it open," I told Ginger. I walked over and closed the door.

On the night before we left, Ginger went to the going away party at my cousin's house. I stayed home to get some sleep. I started to hear noises when Ginger left. Someone was in the house. I heard footsteps, but not those of a man; they were the little footsteps of a child. I had seen my sister's spirit last time we were in Norway, so I figured it was my sister as a young girl. The footsteps were in the kitchen, then the stairs, then in the landing upstairs outside of our bedroom.

"Hey Bjørg," I said, assuming that the ghost was my sister. No response, but the footsteps stopped. Just after we arrived, I had invited the actors over to see the

old house that's the focal point of the play. All the action of the play takes place in a stage set based on our old farmhouse. All the actors were moved to tears being in the real house that they had become so familiar with in its stage incarnation. They looked at the photographs on the wall depicting some of the characters they were portraying in the play.

I invited the actors to sit on the Nazi love couch where the Nazi colonel wooed local Norwegian girls during the war. Some did, but most didn't dare sit on that couch. We took a group picture on the front steps to the house where the Nazi colonel had tortured my great aunt by making her stick her head in the snow because the steps were not kept clear for him. I'm sure most of the student actors felt the presence of my departed family members in the house. My own epiphany, as it turned out, was truly realizing the healing power of my parents' story and sharing that with others through my play. I've rediscovered my roots and taken responsibility for passing on Norwegian cultural traditions to the next generations in our family. My dream was realized by bringing *The Epiphany* home to Norway where it belongs. Dreams can be real.

EPILOGUE

I met Holocaust survivor George Brown in 2003 when he and his wife came to visit my World War II history class at Citrus College. George gave a very moving witness account of his imprisonment at Auschwitz. He lost his entire family in the Holocaust. A remarkable man and a tragic story. In the epilogue to his book *I Survived the Nazis Hell*, he wrote:

"As my life is passing by me, I can see in front of me my mother; my father; my brothers and sister; my relatives; my friends. All of them died at Auschwitz. As time went by, you would think that it would all become more distant; instead, their faces are coming closer and closer to me. It seems to me now that I was looking through a window in the pouring rain and suddenly the rain stops and the picture becomes very sharp."

Mr. Brown not only had to suffer personally in a concentration camp, but he also had to suffer through losing his whole family as well. Then, as if that wasn't bad enough, he had to carry with him the story and the endless retelling and exposure of his grief. All of this was tinged with some survivor's guilt. Although the story of what the Nazis did to George Brown and his family during the Holocaust is heartbreaking, horrific, and vitally important to study and learn from, what intrigues me most about his story is that George felt closer to his departed family as he grew older and drew nearer to his own death. We all would like to believe that when we die, we'll be reunited with our loved ones. It's a comforting thought. George Brown sensed that his reunion with departed loved ones was imminent. He died in 2010, less than eight years after he wrote those words.

A Pew Research poll in 2009, found that 18 percent of the respondents had seen a ghost. A Huffington Post/YouGov poll in

2012, found that 45 percent believed in ghosts. That's a significant number of people. As for skeptics, I understand their doubts. If you have not experienced ghosts or any paranormal phenomena and science has struggled to account for the paranormal, skepticism is a logical position to take. But consider this, maybe you have experienced something and were unaware of it. As Leslie Rule (daughter of best-selling true crime author Ann Rule) wrote in her book *Coast to Coast Ghosts*, "…many of us probably have seen ghosts and not even realized it. For instance, that pale teenage girl sitting alone on the bench in the train station or the elderly woman trudging along the side of the road may not be a living being at all. Who actually stops to check each person they encounter?" She noted that there are five signs that the person you see may be a ghost:

1. The person is very pale.
2. When you look away for just a moment, the person is gone.
3. The person ignores you when you try to engage them.
4. The person is located in a strange or unusual location like a deserted road or the window of an abandoned house.
5. The person seems to be wearing anachronistic clothing or is inappropriately dressed for the season.

Now that I've written all of these stories, most of which I hadn't written about before, and some that I hadn't even spoken about before, I realize how important these paranormal events have been to my development as a person. We're the sum total of our experiences. What started out in my life as just blind faith in God instilled by tradition, church, Sunday school, and my parents, has now, through all of my experiences and mistakes and triumphs, become the core of my spiritual life. I had no idea when I set out to write these stories that they would be so important to me and who I am. All of these things have happened for a reason.

I've never really understood why I've been given the gift of seeing and hearing things that most others don't or maybe don't want to acknowledge, but now I think I know. I've had all of these paranormal experiences so that I can tell the story and help others to open up their senses to everything around us.

Ancient people were open to the ethereal world, a world that still exists today. Even though we live in an age of reason and logic, for which I'm grateful, that does not mean that we should shun or ignore our past. Being an historian, I understand all too well the importance of the past, as the future is unknown and the present is fleeting. My main contribution to the study of history has been to stress the importance of the individual in history. As I always tell my students, history begins and ends with the individual. For example, historical events didn't happen to America—they happened to individual Americans. It's individuals who give their lives in armed conflicts and lose their homes during financial downturns. I also ask my students on the first day of class: who are you and why are you here? I believe it's never too early to begin the formal journey of self-discovery. Reading as many different books, articles, and interviews as possible have helped me keep an open mind, broadened my perspective and enhanced my writing, and helped me understand my purpose and role in the world. My writing has helped me chart my way through life and stay on course.

One of my favorite writers was Ray Bradbury. He wrote fantasy, horror, and science fiction stories and books, although he resisted being called a science fiction writer. A few years ago, I was a guest speaker on Veterans Day at the South Pasadena Library. My wife Ginger, my mother-in-law Mary, and I were asked to wait in the Bradbury Room of the library. It was a marvelous room that was dedicated to Ray Bradbury and had many excellent old books in beautiful wood bookcases showcasing pictures of the author. I loved that room and its view of an old twisted Moreton Bay Fig tree outside of the paned windows. He loved that room as well and spent many hours there reading. I was inspired, and later I read an interview with Ray Bradbury where he mentioned his inspiration for writing.

On Labor Day week of 1932 in Waukegan, Illinois, after attending the funeral for his favorite uncle, young Ray visited a small carnival and saw a magician named Mr. Electrico. This magician sat in an electric chair and had his assistant flip a switch. Electricity then shot through his body, and his hair stood on end. Then, after thrusting his sword into the air with sparks shooting from its tip, Mr. Electrico knighted young Ray and other awestruck children in the front row with his electric sword. When Mr. Electrico touched Ray's forehead with the electric sword, he shouted: "Live Forever!" Young Ray was amazed and felt transformed by the experience later saying that he had run from death, in the form of his uncle's funeral, to life. Later, young Ray met Mr. Electrico who introduced him to others in the carnival sideshow including the Illustrated Man, the Fat Lady, the Skeleton Man, the acrobats, and others. Mr. Electrico then told young Ray that he had met him before, in the Great War, and that Ray had been his friend and that he had died in his arms at the Battle of the Ardennes. Mr. Electrico told young Ray that he recognized him as his friend who had come back, reincarnated. Young Ray was moved to tears and felt so inspired that he started writing that day and continued to do so for the rest of his life. Ray Bradbury knew that he could live forever through his writing.

All of my paranormal experiences and education (both formal and informal), has led me to believe that instead of thinking that we're going backward in development by embracing the ancient ethereal world, we should look at it as a re-discovery of something that was lost along the way. We can combine secular enlightenment with paranormal illumination and create a new age of peace.

Paranormal phenomena, once they are shared, better understood, and not feared, could unite all of us all around the world. Then perhaps we can learn to live in peace with our past, our present, and our future simultaneously and seamlessly as my dear departed friend Gene Thorkildsen tried to explain to me after his death.

From my understanding of quantum physics, the reality we see only becomes reality when we observe it. Everything in the universe is entangled in its natural quantum state (matter, energy, and time itself). Our consciousness creates our reality from a quantum field where everything is connected like a soup of molecules and atoms. Many researchers believe that psychic phenomena operate in the realm of the quantum state where everything is entangled, and where we may at times catch a glimpse of it.

Dr. Dean Radin in his book *Entangled Minds* writes: "One of the most surprising discoveries of modern physics is that objects aren't as separate as they may seem. When you drill down into the core of even the most solid-looking material, separateness dissolves. All that remains...are relationships extending curiously throughout space and time." He goes on to say that "...scientists are now finding that there are ways in which the effect of microscopic entanglements 'scale up' into our macroscopic world...tasks can be accomplished by entangled groups without the members of the group communicating with each other in any conventional way. Some scientists suggest that the remarkable degree of coherence displayed in living systems might depend in some fundamental way on quantum effects like entanglement." Quantum theorist Wolfgang Pauli said that: "It is my personal opinion that in the science of the future, reality will neither be psychic nor physical but somehow both and somehow neither."

Dr. Radin goes on to point out that physics is the study of the objective universe, but it's known only through our subjective consciousness. "Could consciousness be a fundamental force in the universe that binds and shapes how the universe manifests? It might be the glue that holds everything together and creates something rather than nothing." So, we're all connected to each other and the world and the universe just as ancient people, spiritual leaders, and mystics have always told us.

We've come to the end of this book, dear reader. However, I hope it's not the end of our journey of discovery. I'm reminded of a passage in Vietnam War helicopter pilot Robert Mason's book *Chickenhawk: Back in the World*: "There's an ancient idea that when a man travels, he doesn't *go* anywhere. Instead, he performs a series of actions that, if done in the proper sequence, will bring his destination to him." For me, writing this book and sharing my personal paranormal history was the action I needed to take to reach my destination. I've learned through my many years of studying war and conflict that the easiest way to control people is through fear or anger. When a person is angry or afraid, they aren't as smart as when they are calm. With that in mind, I would like to return to my earlier idea that there are forks in the road of time. If it's true that we die many times and live on in other alternate paths as ourselves until we finally reach old age and then die only to be reincarnated, what do we have to fear? As I wrote earlier, if death really is the ultimate deception, then we would no longer have a fear of death controlling and limiting us. We would be indeed *timeless*.

I hope I've inspired you, dear reader, to embrace the unknown, and use all of your senses, and not be afraid of the paranormal events in your life. We don't have to let others make us angry or afraid, and we don't have to wait for others to tell us what to believe or what not to believe. We have our individual experiences to teach us and guide us. There is a universe of knowledge yet to be learned, and we're only scratching the surface. I wish you all to love one another, live well, and live forever!

ABOUT THE AUTHOR

Bruce Olav Solheim was born on September 3, 1958, in Seattle, Washington, to hard-working Norwegian immigrant parents, Asbjørn and Olaug Solheim. Bruce was the first person in his family to go to college. He served for six years in the US Army as a jail guard and later as a helicopter pilot. He earned his PhD in history from Bowling Green State University in 1993.

Bruce is currently a distinguished professor of history at Citrus College in Glendora, California. He also served as a Fulbright Professor in 2003 at the University of Tromsø in northern Norway.

Bruce founded the Veterans Program at Citrus College and cofounded, with Manuel Martinez and Ginger De Villa-Rose, the Boots to Books transition course—the first college course in the United States designed specifically for recently returned veterans. He has published eight books and has written ten plays, two of which have been produced.

Bruce is married to Ginger, the girl of his dreams, who is a professional helicopter pilot and certified flight instructor. He has been blessed with four wonderful children: Bjørn, Byron, Caitlin, and Leif. He also has two precious grandsons, Liam and Wesley. Bruce, his brother, and his nephew still own the family home in Åse, Norway, two hundred miles above the Arctic Circle.

ABOUT THE ARTIST

Gary Dumm is a life-long Cleveland resident and artist who worked with Harvey Pekar on *American Splendor* since Pekar began self-publishing that comic 42 years ago. He has shown artwork in exhibitions nationally from Cleveland to San Francisco and internationally from Canada to Germany. His cartoons have been shown in *Entertainment Weekly*, the *New York Times*, the *Village Voice* and France's *le Monde* and in *Cleveland Scene*, *Free Times* and *Plain Dealer*.

Currently, Gary writes and draws pieces for *Music Makers Rag* (biographies of blues musicians helped by that organization out of North Carolina) and juggles several graphic novel projects. His talented wife, Laura, adds color to his work as required, allowing him to do that much more in black and white.

BLURBS

Timeless by Bruce Solheim is an amusing and instructive account of the visionary experiences of the author. This man is a natural born story teller! Each chapter is self-contained and reads like a present-day fairy tale, but cumulatively the chapters also tell the story of the life of a flawed but charming and sincere human being, with an uncanny knack for witnessing paranormal events and recounting them with cinematic vividness. A skeptic will be inclined to dismiss these accounts of paranormal experiences as either fabrications or self-deceiving surrender to an overwrought imagination, but the ultimate effect of reading this book is to provoke a skepticism about the skepticism. If skepticism is just a confession of lack of knowledge, then why is the skeptic so sure that such weird events can't possibly happen? This book raises important questions about the relations between the spiritual and the physical and is entertaining to boot! Highly recommended.

Jack Call, Ph.D.
Philosophy Professor (retired), Citrus College and author

The modern scientific world has no patience for the "paranormal." High strangeness experiences are explained away as dumb luck, coincidence, or misperception. Surely, we're told, no educated person could possibly believe in telepathy, spirits, ghosts, or magic. But in a spellbinding series of true vignettes in the life of college professor Bruce Olav Solheim, the paranormal is vibrantly alive. *Timeless* is not about belief. It's about genuine experiences that science has yet to understand. Highly recommended.

Dean Radin, Ph.D.
Chief Scientist, Institute of Noetic Sciences
Distinguished Professor, California Institute of Integral Studies
President of Parapsychological Association

I enjoyed every word of *Timeless*. The book presents wonderful stories from beyond the reach of what we like to think of as reality. Bruce is a gifted story teller, for sure. Nobody else writes stories like he does.

David A. Willson,
U.S. Army veteran of the Vietnam War
Retired reference librarian and professor
Vietnam War literature and film bibliographer, and author

CPSIA information can be obtained
at www.ICGtesting.com
Printed in the USA
LVHW052135160222
711308LV00016B/2296